MUSIC FOR
PEOPLE WITH
LEARNING DISABILITIES

HUMAN HORIZONS SERIES

MUSIC FOR
PEOPLE WITH
LEARNING DISABILITIES

MIRIAM WOOD

A CONDOR BOOK
SOUVENIR PRESS (E & A) LTD

First published 1983 under the title
Music for Mentally Handicapped People
by Souvenir Press (Educational & Academic) Ltd,
43 Great Russell Street, London WC1B 3PA
and simultaneously in Canada

Reprinted 1993 (retitled)

ISBN 0 285 63155 1

Printed in Great Britain by
The Guernsey Press Co. Ltd, Guernsey, Channel Islands.

CONTENTS

Foreword   9

Acknowledgments   11

Introduction   13

1 **But I am not a Musician**   19
   The ability to relate   20
   Share what you have   21
   Learn to play an instrument   22
   Your singing voice   26
   Keep trying   27

2 **Aims of Music Activities**   28
   Responses grow   29
   Skills develop   29
   New skills are learnt   30
   Long term aims   30
   Goal planning   32

3 **What Shall I Need?**   34
   Enthusiasm   34
   Patience   35
   A plan of action   36
   A room   37
   Instruments   38
   Make your own instruments   41

4 **Enjoyment One-to-One**   46
   Reasons for individual sessions   47
   Music activities   48
   Motivation   51
   Exercises for those in wheelchairs   57
   Music through the day   62
   Learning to read and play music   64

Improvisation   65
'Conversation' on a drum   67
Strumming a guitar   68

5 **Group Music Making**   69
   Seating   69
   Let's enjoy ourselves   70
   What shall we do?   71
   Ability of pupils   91
   Additional activities   93

6 **Listening to Music**   98
   Recorded music versus live music   98
   Variety of music   98
   Reaction to music   99
   A calming influence   100
   A record club   100
   Something to avoid   101

7 **Let's Write Songs**   102
   How to write songs   102
   Examples of songs   104
   Writing songs with your pupils   124
   The Makaton Vocabulary   126
   Makaton songs   127

8 **Music to Move**   134
   Exploring patterns for group movement   134
   Including pupils in wheelchairs   142
   Frequency and duration of sessions   143
   Individual movement for physically handi-
   capped pupils   143
   Folk dancing   143
   Wheelchair dancing   146
   Educational Rhythmics   148

9 **Drama and Music**   152
   Acting out a story   152
   Sounds   153
   Vocal imitations of instruments   154
   Sound into action   155
   Drama productions   155

10   **Music in Worship**   177

In Conclusion   183

Reading List and Song Books   185

Useful Addresses   189

FOREWORD

The role of music and the arts as applied to the treatment of handicapped people is becoming steadily more important. The general philosophy that treatment is effective when this brings pleasure to the patient has changed many of the involvements which take place in every kind of therapy. Music is no exception; indeed it has a special place because of the special pleasure which musical experiences bring to those handicapped people whose powers of communication are limited or undeveloped. The provision of Music Therapists is yet sparse and many of those who are concerned with the management of handicapped people and who help to bring pleasure into their lives could do this more effectively if they could harness the musical interests of their pupils, but often a lack of skill or confidence acts as a barrier to their attempts.

Miriam Wood has addressed herself to this group of interested but untrained people and she has done so in a readable and direct way. She covers the practical needs for an effective approach, illustrates the reactions which might be expected and draws attention to the underlying principles. Her approach is lucid and it will appeal to parents and all those who work directly with handicapped people.

Franz S. Morgenstern M.A., D.P.M., D.M., M.R.C.Psych.
Consultant Psychiatrist

To Cecilia Henry and all my handicapped friends.

ACKNOWLEDGMENTS

The author thanks all those who have aided her in sharing music with handicapped people:

The Berkshire Area Health Authority (prior to reorganisation) for aid from the Scholarship Fund (1978); Mr Paul Walsh and Mr Graham Clarke.

The staff of Church Hill House Hospital, Bracknell, Berkshire, in particular Mr C. Harris, Administrator, East Berkshire Health Authority, Mr W. Henning, Director of Nursing Services, Mr D. Moffat, Training Officer, Mrs G. Lovell, Unit Sister, and the staff in the Social Training Unit and other areas of the hospital; Alan Norvill, my first partner in presenting music activities, my former 'right hand' Patricia Patrick and my present assistant Julie Garraway.

Penny Sanderson, drama teacher, for the privilege of working with her and her help in preparing this book; Tim Naylor, for his music during the drama sessions; Ann Varma, drama and movement teacher, for a happy working relationship of several years and for sharing her ideas on folk dancing; Peggy Pritchett, speech therapist, for her help and encouragement and for allowing me to use her version of 'The Sleeping Beauty'; Jean Cooper, former occupational therapist at the hospital, for her support during a difficult time and the production of 'The Sleeping Beauty'.

Paul Williams, Castle Priory College, for encouraging me to share my ideas with others; Daphne Kennard, Music Advisor, the Disabled Living Foundation, for aid in compiling the address and reading list and for her support over the years; Janet Wyatt, Training Unit, the City Lit., for arranging for those using music with handicapped people to meet and share ideas; David Ward, Dartington College, for sharing his knowledge and his advice; Peter Flockhart, musician, for his aid with the songs in this book and for providing the harmony.

Sarah Applin and Sally-Ann Jolliffe of Edgebarrow School, Crowthorne, for their song 'Teeth Cleaning'; James Gilford for his beautiful photographs and for his patience and love of handicapped people; Margaret Walker, Makaton Development Project, for allowing the use of material regarding Makaton Sign Vocabulary; Jennet Robins, Switzerland, for permission to quote from *Educational Rhythmics for Mentally and Physically Handicapped Children*; Shirley Moule, Educational Rhythmics Department, BIMH, for her practical help; Helen Newman for allowing me to quote extensively from her dissertation prepared for her final year at the City of Liverpool College of Higher Education; Nina Miller for her 'recipe' for making drums quoted from her book; Joy Hornsby, student nurse at Borocourt Hospital, Reading, for her delightful illustrations; Oxford University Press for permission to quote from *Music for the Handicapped Child* (2nd edition) by Juliette Alvin.

Bracknell College for a space in which to work and the use of a typewriter on several occasions, and Church Hill House Hospital for the use of a typewriter.

And finally, Leslie, John and Tanya, my family, for their help on occasions and for being so long-suffering while I write.

INTRODUCTION

What music means to you and me

The term 'music' covers so many things. It is produced by arranging and combining sounds to form something beautiful (or sometimes not so beautiful) that expresses our emotions. We think of bird song, the sound of a babbling brook, wind blowing through the trees, a mother's lullaby to her baby, a symphony orchestra, Scottish pipers, children's singing games, music for a ballet or an opera, jazz, rock music – and so I could go on, referring to what we term music and musical sound.

Music has played a prominent role throughout man's history. Instrumental music certainly sounded different in past centuries and vocal styles have changed too, but each generation and nation has developed its own form. Almost everyone derives pleasure from music and chooses to listen to his or her chosen style; even those who do not seek it out find that it is never far from them – whether in supermarkets, television advertisements, background music to films or the chimes of the ice cream van!

In this book I want to encourage you to think about the music you enjoy and for you to consider how you can share music with people in your care who have learning disabilities. We shall explore the ways in which they can experience joy and through music express their feelings so that they may develop and have a chance to reach their full potential in life.

Music in my life

Music has always had a special place in my life. I am told that I entered the world to the song of a blackbird outside the window of the room where I was born! My mother recalls that when only a few days old I turned my head and listened intently to music on the radio. Of course I remember nothing of this, but as I grew older music certainly played an important role in my life. Born in Wales, the 'Land of Song', everything was celebrated with music; my mother was a pianist and singer and my father a non-musician but with a natural singing voice; I was encouraged to sing solos from about the age of four; there was Saint David's Day and its musical events, Welsh choirs and chapel congregations. Breathing and music were synonymous.

Music and emotion
Some of the finest singing you will ever hear is at a Welsh funeral. When Grandfather died the chapel was packed to the doors and the congregation sang from their hearts the hymns they all loved. I realised that music can express feelings that words alone can never say. As a teenager I found expression for my inmost joys and fears that I could barely understand, let alone describe, through piano music, the deep tones of the organ, or violin melodies.

Have you noticed the part that music plays in your life? Your experience is inevitably different from mine, but as you think it over perhaps you will be surprised by the way it has enriched your daily life – even if you by no means consider yourself a musician.

A journey into music with learning disabled people
I heard about Richard some time before I met him, as other staff at the Children's Home chatted about him. He was in hospital for yet another operation so I had known nothing of him during my first weeks with the children. I asked some questions about him, only to be told, 'Just wait till next week and then you'll know *all* about him.'

He burst upon the scene a few days later – a small thin boy about seven years old with blond wispy baby hair, tiny slits for eyes, ears that had been made for him during the course of his operations and legs that rarely stopped running. I quickly began to know all about him. 'Over active' was an understatement to describe him. Without drugs he would have continued his speedy flight to nowhere without a pause for rest. Even with drugs he slept for only a few hours at night and the havoc he created climbing on top of wardrobes or turning on taps and causing a flood late at night, or waking everyone at the crack of dawn by playing with the staff cups and saucers, is a story in itself.

Yet occasionally he did stop: at meal times he sat and ate heartily until he had finished everything in sight or was told firmly that he had had quite enough – and he stopped for music. If someone turned on the record player he would appear from nowhere and sit with his ear to the speaker listening intently until the music ceased.

How I longed to enjoy music with him and help him to form relationships rather than live in his own small world with little regard for other people. But although I shared his enjoyment, I did not know how to relate to him through music and could only think in terms of teaching him to play an instrument.

Later I began working with adults who had learning disabilities and one of the first areas in which I became involved was music. Someone with little musical knowledge or skill had also realised its value, so together we worked to develop a programme specifically for adults with learning disabilities. This presented a challenge to us. The people with the least disability gained a tremendous amount from music; they responded in a very positive way and were readily able to play music together. Those with most disabilities had to be considered carefully and methods tried and accepted or rejected through experience.

Consideration and respect

We learned a great deal as we worked with our pupils; they taught us as much as we taught them. They told us verbally or non-verbally of their likes and dislikes in music; we realised our need to treat each person as an individual, with equal rights, and we learned to see the potential in someone and to work to bring it out. We shared our love of music with them and they with us, and together we developed understanding and respect one for the other.

Can everyone be involved?

Through the years, I have found that there are very few people who are unable to benefit from a programme of music. It can be extremely difficult to work with certain people with learning disabilities: they may present all kinds of additional problems such as hyperactivity, incontinence, aggressive behaviour, lack of concentration and so on; yet most pupils with such problems can still benefit from music sessions. Pupils with learning disabilities who are confined to wheelchairs are sometimes less difficult to cope with – although programme content has to be considered carefully – as at least they are not trying to run away!

Students with visual disabilities often excel at music, as listening for sounds is part of their everyday life. Also having learning disabilities may limit what they can do, but most pupils with visual disabilities are able to make some progress in learning to sing or to play an instrument. Pupils with hearing disabilities need not be excluded from music either, for although hearing is the main requisite for enjoyment, vibrations are produced by musical notes which can be felt. Most people with hearing disabilities can hear at least some tones; even people with no hearing may be able to excel at such activities as dancing and playing instruments. When a pupil has learning disabilities as well as a hearing loss it is more difficult to ascertain the degree of hearing disability and may increase reluctance to wear a hearing aid. Even so, each person can be observed to see how he can benefit from the use of music.

Pupils without speech are at a disadvantage in being unable to respond verbally to music or to sing songs. If they are being taught a sign language or vocabulary, songs using signs can be introduced into music sessions to enable them to take a more active role in the programme. Some people with learning disabilities have no speech or have speech which is difficult to understand. Playing an instrument can be used as a means of expressing their feelings by making sounds that they are usually incapable of making themselves. On instruments they can simulate a conversation, or can express anger, joy or other emotions.

Pupils confined to wheelchairs can enjoy a variety of musical activities by playing instruments using those parts of the body that are able to move. Some instruments can be adapted for use by people with physical disabilities, and it is a very satisfying experience for such pupils to be able to sing or play an instrument. If a young person can join an orchestra, choir, band or group on an equal basis with able bodied friends, or together with other people with various disabilities, it can be a great boost to morale.

Of autistic children Juliette Alvin writes:
'Autistic symptoms affect the whole learning process and create deep obstacles to the development of human relationships . . . He [the child] lacks warmth, is aloof and cold, either withdrawn or hyperactive. He seems to live in a closed world, which may be a refuge or a prison . . .

'The way the autistic child relates to his environment is reflected in his reactions to music. Music or sounds have the power to penetrate and may break down his defences, thus provoking communication. Music can create a non-verbal, non-threatening environment in which the child can express himself.' (*Music for the Handicapped Child*, pages 107–8. See Reading List for details.)

Having any type of disability need not exclude a pupil from enjoyment derived from music. Individual difficulties may create problems but these can usually be overcome by careful planning, forethought and by time and patience.

Anyone living or working with people who have learning disabilities may like to try the ideas in this book. It was written to encourage those who enjoy music, to whatever degree, to share it in a meaningful way and to go on to develop their own ideas. It does not describe music therapy, as that is a field which requires a high standard of musicianship and specific training at postgraduate level.

Since this book was published in 1983 terminology has changed. The title and introduction have been altered at the time of reprinting but it has not been possible to update outmoded phrases or terminology throughout the entire book. I hope that this does not detract from the purpose of the book or create misunderstandings.

1:   BUT I AM NOT A MUSICIAN

You are obviously interested in music and its uses with handicapped people.Perhaps you are already enjoying music activities with your pupils, or you are planning to become involved. You may be a competent musician seeking further ways of using your musical skill to bring music to your child or pupils; or else you may have a little knowledge of music and need advice and reassurance in using it successfully to aid those who are handicapped.

Whatever your interest in the subject, in this chapter I want to pay particular attention to those who do not feel that they are musicians, who have little or no ability to play an instrument, do not sing well and have scant knowledge of reading music. If you fall into this category you may feel that it will be little use trying to teach pupils something that you have not mastered yourself. You are not a musician, fair enough, but as I mentioned in the introduction, music has an effect on everyone and we have the ability to enjoy it whether or not we can play an instrument or sing ourselves. It is difficult to find people who state that they actively dislike all kinds of music.

So, you are not a musician, but perhaps you could refer to yourself as musical? A song or a piece of music conjures up for you memories of a particular day, a happy occasion (or even a sad one), someone you used to know, or a place you visited. You relax as you listen to your favourite music after a hard day at work or caring for your family; a signature tune calls you to watch your favourite television programme; you hum a television commercial as you go about your work; music from a film reminds you of the story and your mind recalls the happy and sad events in it. You hear a children's hymn and you are back in Sunday school; a nursery rhyme and you see yourself sitting on a tiny chair experiencing the big new world of your first day at school.

The ability to relate

Whatever your involvement with a handicapped person, it is of
prime importance that you should be able to relate to him. You
may have the most wonderful programme in the world, have
the best instruments and the latest equipment at your disposal
and may even have won prizes in music. All of these are of no
avail if you cannot relate to your child or pupils. It is
immaterial whether they are physically handicapped or mildly,
moderately or severely mentally handicapped, your pupils will
know if you are really interested in them, wanting to share
something with them and enthusiastically leading them
towards satisfaction and success or fulfilment. They will sense
if you are just going through the motions of an activity while
looking forward to the next break, the end of the day, or pay
day. Those who are able to voice their opinion may express
their feelings to someone else by saying, 'She doesn't like me,'
or 'She couldn't care less,' or worse still, 'I hate her.' Those who
do relate well to handicapped people are sought out by pupils
for understanding at times when all the world seems against
them. During activity sessions the most withdrawn pupils will
usually work well and confidently with staff who have built up
a relationship and understanding with them.

It is not difficult to recognise someone who is willing to
relate well. Directly he enters a room where there are
handicapped people engaged in an activity it is possible to
observe him and tell whether he is willing to relate to them or
not:

1. He shows interest in the activity and the people involved.
2. He is willing to join in but is not 'pushy'.
3. He does not sit down and allow a glazed look to pass over
    his eyes, nor does he start up a conversation over the heads
    of the pupils about a totally different subject.
4. He takes note of the activity in hand and aids the pupils to
    participate without taking over the role of teacher or pupil.
5. He is thinking carefully, observing both teacher and pupils
    and taking an intelligent interest in what is going on.
6. He never laughs *at* the pupils but laughs *with* them.

The ability to relate well and develop empathy with your
pupils is vital to the success or failure of your music activities

with them. You are sharing something with them that you both enjoy. This has an advantage over some other activities which may not have the same immediate attraction. It is possible to feel very close to your pupils with music as the shared activity. I enjoy a togetherness with my pupils at these times. As I concentrate on them through the medium of music I develop an understanding of their feelings, fears, problems and joys as they find expression for their emotions through music. I work to bring out the beauty I find in them or aid them to overcome through music their anger, frustration or imaginary fears. It is not easy for others to realise exactly what is happening during music sessions if they are not fully involved in the programme themselves, or have not allowed themselves to absorb the atmosphere created at these times. Something very special happens when teacher and pupil are involved in listening to or making music together. It is a combination of single-mindedness in a shared activity and true regard and respect for handicapped people as individuals and equals. It is, after all, but an accident of birth that you are the teacher and he the pupil, that you are regarded as 'normal' and he as 'handicapped'. Put yourself in his place and treat him as you would wish to be treated if your roles were reversed.

Share what you have
What we have just been considering is sharing ourselves with our pupils. Now let's think in terms of music. What can you share with your pupils if you fall into the category of non-musician? Assess your own ability and make a list of the musical activities in which you are able to take part:

1. Can you sing, even a little?
2. Have you ever learned to play any musical instruments?
3. Did you play in a percussion band at school or use an instrument during class music sessions?
4. Can you read music?
5. Do you enjoy listening to music, recorded or live?

If you lack confidence, begin by sharing with your pupils a musical activity that you most enjoy and with which you are familiar. As your confidence grows you can then broaden your scope to include other aspects which at first you might have found difficult.

Learn to play an instrument

You may never have tried to learn to play an instrument, but it is never too late to begin; although it may take a while to get the idea initially it is not difficult in the long term. You will need to persevere through the first difficult weeks or months. Some instruments, such as the harp, flute, violin or pipe organ, are more complicated to play than others, so choose something easier such as the piano or guitar.

A short cut to playing an instrument, or one to play while learning another instrument, is the autoharp (also called a chordal dulcimer or chromaharp). This instrument only requires you to press a button and strum the strings in order to provide a chordal accompaniment for songs. Your pupils may also be able to use this instrument.

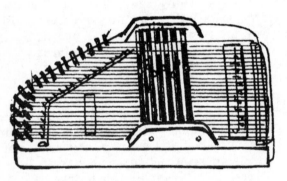

An autoharp

Learn to play a few chords on a guitar. If possible join an evening class in order to learn, or seek someone's aid to teach you to tune the guitar and to read the positions of chords on a chart. You will find it very difficult for your fingers at first, but quickly, depending on how much time you are prepared to spend practising, you will improve (see chord chart).

If you have never had the opportunity to take piano lessons you may think of it as an instrument totally out of your range,

CHORD CHART – BASIC CHORDS FOR GUITAR

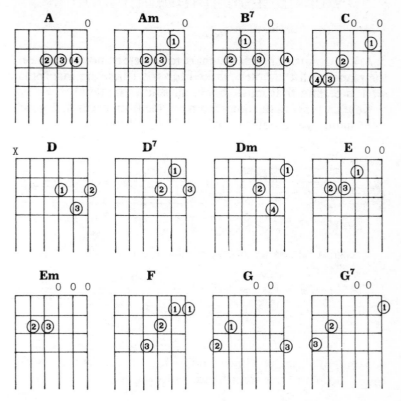

0 = open string to play
X = not to be played

unless you are blessed with the ability to play by ear. Many people who cannot play the piano have a desire to learn or wish they had agreed to have lessons when they were young. Do not be put off by your lack of knowledge. It is possible that you can learn to play sufficiently for your needs. If you know nothing at all about the piano, ask someone who does to show you where middle C is. Mark it with a sticker and name the white notes up the scale (eight notes or an octave) to octave C. These are all the notes you need to learn as they are repeated up and down the piano.

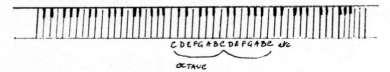

Ask at a music shop for a chart to place behind the keys on the piano with the notes marked for you (these are incorporated in certain first music books or sold separately).

Now try playing the notes from middle C upwards with your right hand, white notes only:

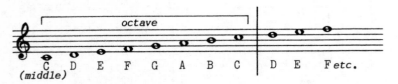

Use your left hand to play the bass notes up to middle C:

Think of a tune you know and try to pick out the melody on the piano with your right hand. For example:

WHEN THE SAINTS

Try other tunes, or choose a beginner's book and write the letter names under the notes. Play them until you are able to recognise the notes by themselves without the need for writing them underneath.

Some tunes you may try to play do not sound right if played only on the white notes. At the point where the tune sounds incorrect, use the black note immediately to the right or left of the white note you are playing. The black note to the right will make the sound slightly higher (sharpen – ♯) and the one to the left will make the sound slightly lower (flatten – ♭).

For example:

HAPPY BIRTHDAY

flatten (♭)
the notes.

You can play the notes of the melody with the left hand at the same time as you play it with the right hand, but an octave lower (8 notes) in order to give it more body. You can play for yourself to sing in this way or accompany your pupils successfully.

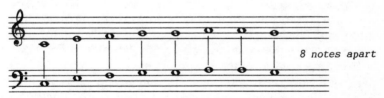

8 notes apart

Perhaps you would like to add chords instead to harmonise with the melody. For example:

Sit and experiment with notes and chords on the piano and you will begin to find what sounds right and what does not. Although I could already read music and play the piano, I found that having to play from music made me lose contact with my pupils and I had to learn to memorise melodies and add bass chords and to make up melodies and provide a chordal accompaniment.

If you do not have access to a piano there are electronic key boards on the market that are played through an amplifier (you may be able to use the amplifier belonging to stereo equipment – but make certain that this is suitable before you connect it).

A chord organ does some of the work for you. The melody is played with the right hand and buttons to use with the left hand provide the appropriate chords. Books of songs are available written to correspond with the particular chord organ you purchase. The correct fingers to use for the melody are also marked. You may be able to teach some of your pupils to play a chord organ, as it is easier than the piano. It could be useful to someone who has limited use of the left hand. He may be able to press the chord buttons even if he is unable to use individual fingers of the left hand.

Your singing voice
'What voice?' you may ask. 'Me sing? You must be joking!' Is it really as bad as that? I am sure that even if you say that you never sing, you could think of occasions when you have burst into song. The best place to practise traditionally is in the bath (I am not sure that a shower has quite the same effect).

If you are not sure of the range of your voice, test it out with a piano. Play middle C and sing it. Try singing upwards one note at a time, as high as feels easy without any strain. Sing down from middle C and see how far you can sing comfortably. If you are a man with a low voice you will probably find that you are in fact singing an octave lower. If you sing within your range, at the same time playing the melody between middle C and octave C (some songs will include one or two notes above or below these notes) your pupils will most likely sing within their own range without any problems.

Keep trying

'If at first you don't succeed . . .' Don't give up and say that you are hopeless before you have really tried. It is worth persisting for a long period. For example, I found that my fingers would not respond when I first attempted to learn to play chords on the guitar. My fingers hurt as I pressed the strings and I gave up the attempt. Later I joined an evening class and mastered a few chords but had to stop in between chords to find the next. It annoyed me that I could not do what I wanted with my fingers, so I again gave up. Later I began to use the guitar with my pupils. They were appreciative of the songs and did not mind if I stopped singing, changed the chord and then continued. Very soon my fingers began to move to the correct strings and I could sing songs the whole way through without a pause.

So whatever you are trying to do – sing, play the piano, guitar or another instument of your choice – remember that if you keep trying (short periods and often are most effective) you are bound to improve.

2: AIMS OF MUSIC ACTIVITIES

Music appeals to most people, handicapped or not, and this attraction can be utilised for the benefit of your handicapped pupils. When they show an immediate interest in what you are doing or using you are in an excellent position to begin teaching them. Their attention is the first requirement. You want to use music to aid them in their everyday lives; it will gain their attention and hold it, and through the medium of music you will be able to teach them what you want them to learn.

When you begin to analyse what you can teach through music you may be very surprised how wide an area of learning it can cover. It is a good idea to sit down and work out what your aims are and how you are to achieve them. In my own case, music sessions had been in operation for some time before anyone stopped to think about the purpose of it all. The reason for this was that the pupils were very severely mentally handicapped and we were not at first sure of their ability to develop through the use of music. Then results began to appear. As we saw what could happen it seemed a good idea to take time to think about the achievements, how they were obtained and how other pupils could be aided likewise. It is best to have aims in mind and work to a plan but at the same time remembering that each pupil is an individual and will not progress at the same speed as others, nor respond equally to the same activity.

Most people think of music in terms of learning to play an instrument. For able children the main aim is for them to learn to read music, play an instrument and reach as high a standard as possible. As a child I had visions of becoming a famous violinist and playing as soloist with an orchestra. Many parents urge their children to practise hard so that they may pass their exams. Your handicapped pupils may be unable to learn to play in this way because of a number of different physical or mental handicaps. Yet this does not prevent them from enjoying and participating in music programmes designed specially for them, or from learning and developing through this involvement.

Many programmes are based on behaviour modification which involves strict discipline. Music can achieve these aims creatively as it is a strong motivator. You will have the spontaneous co-operation of your pupils and they will learn and develop naturally and instinctively while enjoying a pleasurable activity.

Some of the most important things that your pupils learn through music are not easily measured. For example, an increasing love of music which brings joy into their lives, or confidence which is built up through familiarity with a planned music programme, and by their achievements, however small they may be.

Responses grow
Enjoyment of music develops as your pupils are regularly exposed to the music programmes you provide. They may not previously have heard a wide variety of music. They may not have realised before that they are able to sing or may have felt too shy to try because they have been told that they cannot sing in tune. It may be a new experience for them to be given an instrument on which they can make interesting sounds. As they take part in music sessions they will begin to develop a natural pitch and rhythm and a new dimension will be added to their lives.

Skills develop
Delay in the development of basic skills is common in handicapped pupils, and as a result the over-all development is checked as well. Such things as hand-eye co-ordination, eye contact and the co-ordinated use of both hands, are extremely important. If your pupils cannot use their bodies efficiently in order to balance, walk or move in a rhythmic and co-ordinated manner, they are at an immediate disadvantage in performing everyday activities and exploring the world around them.

When an instrument is played to a pupil, he is attracted by the sound it makes. He will think it is fun to hold a beater or drumstick or press notes in order to make these sounds for himself. In order to do this he must look at his hands to see what he is doing to make the sound. When you sing to him he will look at you and learn to make eye contact. Although he may never have used both his hands together to perform tasks, the challenge of using two drum sticks or both hands on a key board will lead to the co-ordinated use of his hands.

New skills are learnt
During music sessions you can introduce many different things that your pupils need to learn. They will enjoy this so much that they will not notice that you are teaching them. For example, you want your pupils to broaden their vocabulary to include the names of the foods they eat, the clothes they wear, parts of their body, colours or the days of the week. When these are presented to them in the form of lively songs, or are acted and sung to music, they take on a new appearance and become a game which is easily remembered. The pill so hard to swallow is now sugar coated and very desirable.

Long term aims
Listed below are some long term aims for music activities. Some pupils may achieve them rapidly, others may be very slow or achieve only one or two aims to a limited degree. Other pupils may not achieve anything which can be measured, but who can tell what joy has entered their lives through the atmosphere created by the music?

1. *Communication and awareness*
   To encourage eye contact with others during singing or instrumental sessions.
   To aid the development of pre-speech or encourage the use of language through making sounds or singing songs.
   To develop a melodic response through singing and playing pitched instruments which will in turn aid speech.
   To develop a rhythmic response through the use of rhythm instruments and rhythmic movements which will aid speech (word rhythms), balance, agility and movement in general.
   To develop awareness of others through the use of name songs.

2. *Co-ordination*

To develop or improve hand-eye co-ordination through the use of instruments.

To aid the co-ordinated use of both hands through the use of instruments (use of two drum sticks, two beaters or both hands on a keyboard).

To aid movement through the co-ordinated use of the body to music.

3. *Educational aims*

To teach pupils to name the clothes they wear, the food they eat and so on, through the use of songs about these subjects, thereby enabling them to make choices for themselves.

To develop body awareness by identifying ears, eyes, feet, toes, etc., through the use of Educational Rhythmics (see page 148).

To increase pupils' concentration span in gradual stages through lengthening their involvement in music sessions.

To improve or develop the concept of numbers and colour recognition through songs about numbers and colours.

To increase awareness of present events, anticipate future events and retain memory of past events through songs related to the present, future and past.

4. *Creative aims*

To develop musical ability, thereby providing a means of expression through improvisation or performance of learned items.

To develop a love of music and the ability to appreciate different styles of music.

To create for the pupils a happy and relaxed atmosphere which provides security for them.

These are just a few of the aims that you may have in mind for your pupils. As they begin to develop their confidence will grow. They will probably not be aware of this but you will notice a difference in their reactions and a willingness to try what they would not have attempted previously. Perhaps this is one of the best reasons for using music, for when confidence grows so many other aims can be achieved.

Something which may surprise you at first is that the ability to enjoy music sessions and to play an active role is not always related to intelligence. Your pupils may have very little ability in many aspects of their lives and yet make large strides forward in music. As a result their self esteem will grow and they will be prepared to tackle things previously thought too difficult for them.

Goal planning

With certain aspects of music sessions it is possible to use goal planning techniques. When you are teaching colours, numbers, the names of the days of the week and so on, you may find it useful to plan the learning in this way. For example, you may wish to teach colour recognition. Make up a song about colour into which various colours will fit (see 'Colour Song', page 119). Sing about one colour only and ask a pupil to identify it each day for one week or two. Then sing about the next colour for a certain period until this is learnt. Make a note of the progress each time the exercise is used. After two colours are well learnt, have a period when both colours are sung about and the correct choice must be made.

Goals that you set for your pupils will be chosen with reference to their ability and the stage of development that they have reached. For example, your pupil may be unable to grasp objects, so your goal will be to teach him this through encouraging him to hold bells, a beater or drumstick. If he can grasp and hold, the next step will be for him to use them – shaking the bells, playing notes using a beater or beating a drum using a drum stick. When he can shake bells, introduce him to shaking them high or low or shaking only when it is his turn to do so and stopping at the correct time. If he plays notes on an instrument it is time to help him to recognise rises and falls in pitch and then to proceed to picking out melodies. If his drum beating is repetitive this will need to be broken down so that he recognises changes in rhythm first by copying and then by initiating rhythmic patterns himself.

You will find it useful to make a list of your pupils' strengths and weaknesses whether or not you choose to use goal planning as part of your music programme. As an example, let us examine the case of Nigel Williams.

Strengths: Nigel is a happy young man. He cannot speak clearly but it is possible to understand some words that he is saying. The speech he has is relevant and he is able to identify his needs fairly well. Nigel is able to walk but his legs and feet are somewhat deformed. He attends music three times a week for an hour each time. He is particularly fond of singing. He does not like holding objects but is attracted to the drum and will hold the drum stick, beat the drum and vary the rhythm.
Weaknesses: Nigel lacks concentration. When he has finished what he wants to do he jumps up and rushes around looking for some fresh distraction and disturbs other pupils. He demands attention by trying to talk about his interests when other pupils are taking their turn with instruments.
Needs: Nigel needs to lengthen his concentration span. He needs to be less self-centred. His speech needs help to develop and improve.

Having listed Nigel's strengths and weaknesses and noted what his needs are, you will be in a better position to plan the programme that will aid his development. To aid his concentration he will need to be involved throughout the music session, so you must make sure that each activity links with the next and that he knows what he is expected to do – for example, sing a certain song, beat the drum, sit and listen, etc. It will help him to think about himself less if he is asked to aid another pupil in some way, such as shaking hands with someone during a welcome song, identifying others during a name song, or by simply being asked to sit next to a pupil to 'look after' him. The use of songs will develop his speech naturally and conversation related to the theme of the songs will also be very helpful. Development of his rhythmic and melodic responses will aid his speech too. Of course if you use a goal planning programme with him you will only work on one aspect at a time in detail.

The other pupils in Nigel's group will also have special needs. When you have listed all their strengths, weaknesses and needs, you will be able to see a pattern and plan a programme around their requirements. In this way progress can be made with each pupil in the group. Music will then not only be appealing to your pupils but will play a very definite role in their development.

3:   WHAT SHALL I NEED?

When commencing a programme of music with pupils it may be difficult to assess what you will need before you actually start. The following requirements are what I have found to be important and may be helpful to you.

Enthusiasm
I place this high on my list of requirements. Without this there will be little progress and you and your pupils will not enjoy what you are doing. If it is your own choice to start a music programme you are probably very enthusiastic already. If it is someone else who has decided that you are exactly the right person to lead out in music sessions, perhaps your enthusiasm needs a gentle prod. It is difficult to be enthusiastic about something thrust upon you by another person and about which you perhaps know very little. If you are expected to both plan and run the programme and there is no one with relevant experience to refer to for help, your enthusiasm may well be low.

But perhaps you are very keen and see music as the best possible way to aid your pupils. Unfortunately there may be other people around you who see no advantage in the use of music and may consider it merely a pastime – or a waste of time. If they have authority over you, you will need sufficient enthusiasm to press on with the programme until you can prove by results that it is in fact valuable (preparation of a list of your aims may aid such people to see the programme in a different light. See Chapter Two, Aims).

During music sessions with your pupils your enthusiasm will spread to them. Make the sessions happy and encouraging times that they look forward to by putting effort into preparing material and energy into sharing it with them.

You will need to be enthusiastic about finding new and

better ways of working with your pupils. In the past this was not always easy, as the number of people actively engaged in music activities with handicapped people, particularly in the field of severely and profoundly mentally handicapped people, was limited. This is now improving and those doing this work need no longer feel a sense of isolation as there is far more communication between those engaged in similar activities. For example, the National Music and Disability Service provides a great deal of useful information and the British Society for Music Therapy continues to promote the benefits of music and bring together those with music in common to share ideas. The Spastics Society runs occasional courses which engender and revitalise enthusiasm amongst qualified musicians and non-musicians. Take advantage of such facilities and also read books on the subject (see Reading List and Useful Addresses).

Try to maintain steady enthusiasm that lasts. A person who turns the world upside down for a few weeks or months and then leaves someone else to continue the project when he or she becomes bored is not what is required.

Patience
Despite the fact that music has power within itself to affect our lives, and although people benefit from its influence, you will need patience when working with your pupils. They will not be miraculously transformed as soon as they become involved in a music programme. You may begin to wonder after a few months why you ever bothered to introduce music. This is when you will need patience to continue working with a particular individual or group of pupils when there seems no point in doing so. A combination of patience and enthusiasm will help you to see hope in the most severely handicapped or difficult pupil. Refuse to accept defeat and choose rather to re-evaluate the situation and perhaps reorganise groups or modify the programme.

Your child or pupils have handicaps which they probably find difficult to live with or fully accept. They are daily learning to develop patience to accept their limitations, and you will need patience to accept their lack of ability and to help them make the most of what they are able to do. It will be necessary with some pupils to try various methods in order to obtain the desired results, and with others you may need to continue doing the same thing over and over again, week after week, if it is to bring the required response. You will need patience to find better methods and to make something repetitive take on fresh meaning each time it is used.

A plan of action
There is little value in beginning a programme without first making a plan. Sit down and think what you are going to do and read all the material available on the subject to give you ideas. If the planning is not yours, discuss it with the planner and examine the reasons for each activity. Decide what you are aiming at and how you hope to achieve it. Once you have work in operation, you will be able to plan goals for each pupil as you observe their individual needs (see Chapter Two, Aims).

Here are some questions that you will find helpful in deciding on a plan of action:

1. What type of handicapping problem are you dealing with and how severely disabled are your pupils?
2. What facilities do you have available?
3. Will your programme consist of music making, singing groups and movement and music sessions, or will you begin with just one aspect initially?
4. What will you organise for those pupils confined to wheelchairs or who spend most of their time lying down?
5. Are you making special provision for deaf or blind pupils?
6. How long will each session last and how often should it be held?
7. Will pupils come in prearranged groups or can you choose group members yourself?
8. Will you have mixed ability groups?
9. What will you do with disruptive pupils who prevent others having a happy and useful time?
10. Will you be able to work with individual pupils at certain times?
11. Who will be assisting you? Is he/she enthusiastic about the programme and happy to work with you and the pupils?

A room

Choosing or finding a room to use may need some negotiation with other people. In your own home you should have little problem unless you have an 'open plan' home or a family who fill the house for most of the time. A multi-purpose room in your home is a suitable place in which to enjoy music with your child. Too often music is thought of as an extra or non essential programme, so a special-purpose room is considered unnecessary; music can be held in odd corners, such as the dining area between meals, a hallway or even a store cupboard. This false idea will make it difficult for sessions to run smoothly and for pupils to progress.

You will need a certain amount of storage space, however limited your equipment. It is helpful to have a designated room so that music equipment can be stored in it and be ready for use.

How large should the room be? For sessions where pupils will be sitting to sing or play instruments you will need a room large enough to accommodate your pupils (not forgetting wheelchairs) but not so big that it encourages them to wander around during sessions. If the room is not too large each pupil will be fairly near to you (some pupils like to have a wall behind them and dislike sitting on a chair in the middle of a room), and their attention will be focused on you rather than on other parts of the room. If there is no room of a suitable size available, perhaps you could arrange for part of a larger room to be screened off in order to concentrate the activity in one area. Of course for music and movement sessions a larger room is preferable.

Try to use a room where there is the least distraction outside the window, such as noisy traffic or a busy footpath. If there is another room beyond it, there will be distraction if people pass to and fro during sessions. It is preferable not to be next door to a kitchen where noise or delectable smells will divert attention. From the point of view of other people using the same building, quiet activities in adjoining rooms may be affected by the constant sound of music, so consider this aspect too.

Perhaps you will be unable to have the exclusive use of a room for music, or you will be involved in a variety of activities with your pupils in the same room throughout the day. In this case perhaps you can store instruments in that room or in a nearby storeroom. Should the ideal room not be available, it is best to begin your programme under less than ideal conditions rather than delay until the conditions are just right. For example, we began music sessions with pupils in a hut, one morning a week, using a few begged and borrowed instruments. Because the programme had become established, when a new training unit opened within a year, a room in it was at once designated for music.

Instruments
The type and number of instruments you need will depend on the ability of your pupils and the size of groups.

1. *One-to-one sessions*
First let's think of what you will need if you are making music one-to-one with your child. It will be very useful to have a piano available, but you can manage without, depending on the activities you propose.

A drum is very useful. Do not be tempted to buy a child's drum that is only a toy. Buy a drum with a good tone. You will find that a large drum is preferable if your child is nearing adult size. It can be placed on the floor or on a low table and will be high enough to beat while the child sits on a chair, or it can be placed at an angle on a chair to aid pupils in wheelchairs to beat it.

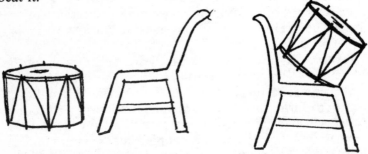

A smaller drum is possibly preferable for a young child, as he may find a large drum frightening both in appearance and sound. An alternative to a drum is a tambour. This is held in the hand and is similar to a tambourine without jingles.

A tambour

A tambourine is also useful as it can encourage your child to use one hand to hold it while tapping on it with the other hand. Sleigh bells make a pleasant sound and encourage a child to grasp and to shake in order to hear the sound.

Your child will benefit by having a xylophone or glocken-spiel, preferably with coloured notes that are not too easily removed. Some children lose interest in playing the instrument when they realise it can be taken apart. As an alternative, individual chime bars can be purchased. They are usually available separately or in sets, which is useful if funds are limited. Use a hard headed beater so that your child does not have to hit the notes hard in order to hear them clearly. He should be encouraged to play with sensitivity rather than to hit them. This may take a while to establish as the initial reaction of some children is to bang as loudly as possible things which respond by making a sound.

You will need an instrument that can be blown. A melodica is quite good as it has notes on it that can be depressed in order to make a melody. This is easier than covering holes on a recorder with the fingers. One melodica on the market has an adaptation for the mouth piece which enables it to be placed on a table and played as a key-board. It can be useful for a child who wants to see clearly which notes he is pressing or for a physically handicapped person who cannot hold it up to his mouth.

A kazoo is an inexpensive item which requires a slightly different approach. It is necessary to hum into it as one does with a comb and paper. It is useful if you are encouraging a child to make sounds as a prerequisite for speech.

A tape recorder can be used to play a variety of music to your child, to record his progress or to encourage him to listen to his performance. Keep a blank tape ready during music sessions

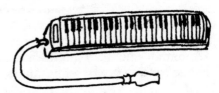

Melodica with adaptation

and record all or at least part of each session. This will encourage you as you are able to refer back and see how your child has progressed over a period of time. It is easy to forget that progress has been made, especially if it is very slow. Encourage him to make sounds to the tape recorder from time to time, or to sing or play an instrument. Some people dry up at the sight of a tape recorder but you may find that your child will sing or play more positively when the tape is played back to him. For example, Malcolm is able to make some sounds and say a few words. He is familiar with the sight of singers on television singing into a microphone, and so when holding a microphone himself he too attempts to sing, and when the recording is played back to him he produces more sounds, trying to compete with his own voice. At other times it is difficult to encourage him to produce either sounds or words. You may find that your child is likewise encouraged to improve his performance by the use of a tape recorder.

2. *Group sessions*
Each of the instruments I have mentioned for use in one-to-one activities will be equally useful with a group. It is possible to work successfully with your pupils with the addition of extra sleigh bells or tambourines, so that there is one for each person to use. When working with a group it will be more important for you yourself to have an instrument to play, as you form the focal point. We began group sessions with a chord organ which enabled my colleague, a non-musician, to play. When that

wore out from constant use we sought a replacement. The music room was too small to accommodate a piano, even if we could have afforded to buy one. We found a second-hand electronic key-board and a local charity purchased it for us from a fund they had set aside to aid handicapped people. I now use a larger room and have a piano which was donated by someone moving house who could not take the piano with him. This leaves the portable key-board free to be used in other locations with pupils who do not come to the music room. If you lack vital equipment and have no funds available it is worth asking for help from a charity, especially one in your immediate locality which may have a personal interest in the pupils and your work.

When purchasing other instruments, what you choose will depend on your group's ability and interests. It is pointless buying expensive instruments if there is no one in the group who can play them. The money would be better spent on buying more percussion instruments that your pupils can really enjoy. Something which is expensive but can be used by pupils of all abilities is a large cymbal on a stand. A good one has a loud but pleasant tone and will need careful looking after to maintain its quality. It can be used in conjunction with a drum for improvised sessions and it is great fun for the pupils to use.

Here is a list of additional instruments which can be purchased in most music shops or ordered through music or school supply catalogues:

Wrist bells, stick bells, cow bells, triangles, maracas, swanee whistles, duck call and bird whistles, recorders, metallaphones, glockenspiels, snare drum on a stand, bongo drums, drum set.

Make your own instruments
It is fairly easy to make your own instruments out of bits and pieces that would otherwise be thrown away. Large empty catering size tins can be made into attractive drums by covering the ends with inner tube rubber and decorating the sides with spare wallpaper or a similar covering.

Nina Miller's book on making instruments (see page 186) gives detailed instructions on how to make a wide variety of instruments including shakers, stick bells, various kinds of rezi-rezi, xylophones, simple stringed instruments and flutes.

These are the details she gives for the making of rubber drums:

> The basic materials are a sturdy tin, some rubber inner tube (car), mason's plumb line and nylon blind cord (No. 2 thickness counting up from the thinnest). A useful size of tin can be obtained from a school or institutional kitchen. Approximate size, diameter 6½" (16.5cm), height 7" (18cm). Some tins have bands or ridges running round the middle. These are good tins to use as the bands make the tins more rigid. Remove the top of the tin, but keep the base in. Check the top edge for sharp bits of metal and tap it flat with a hammer. Any dubious bits can be covered with wallpaper or Fablon at this stage . . . (*details of the best way to cover the tin and the best materials to use*).
>
> The next stage is to cut out the two rubber drum heads. Car and motor cycle inner tubes vary in thickness and elasticity. Once you have cut them open, pull the rubber to test the stretch . . . (*further details regarding the type of tyre and how to prepare it*).
>
> Take your tin and place it on a sound part of the rubber. Use a ball pen to draw around the tin. Remove the tin and draw a second circle on the outside of the first and about 1" (2.5cm) away from it.

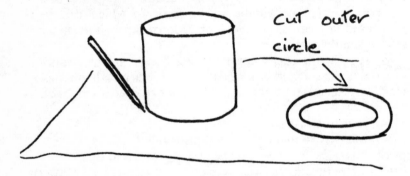

Cut around the outer circle. You may find that you have an oval rather than a circular disc because of the way the rubber curls. You can trim the shape carefully to even it up a bit. Make two discs like this. Halfway between the inner and outer circles mark spots for the holes. Start by marking the 12, 6, 3 and 9 o'clock positions, as this helps to get the spacing even. Put three evenly spaced marks in each quarter. Later on, if you make a larger drum, you may need 4 holes in each quarter. Whatever the number of holes it must be an even total.

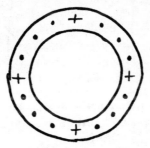

Mark out your second disc in the same way. Use a multihead punch (leather puncher) or a smaller and cheaper single hole punch to punch a hole at each spot. It is very important that these holes are made with a punch. The little round hole it makes does not tear . . .

The next stage is to take a length of mason's plumb line, long enough to lace through the holes and tie, using a reef knot. Before tying the ends pull the plumb line so that the rubber is pulled into a mob cap shape. You can do this more easily if someone else holds the rubber in place on the tin.

With both caps in place, use four odd bits of string to tie the top cap to the base cap. These should just hold the caps firm and level without dragging them to one side or the other. These strings are temporary helpers . . . the real lacing is done with nylon blind cord. It zig-zags from top to bottom cap, so you can work out how much you need: approximately 3 yards (2.75 metres) for a drum this size.

 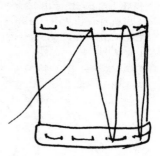

Thread the cord through the plumb line loops. Don't put any real tension on the cord at this stage. The caps should just be held together firmly . . .

The next stage of tightening the lacing is best done standing at a table. You are going to take up the slack in easy stages. If you pull very tight in one go you will probably end up with the caps slipping to one side.

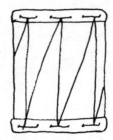

If you have a group of pupils who are able to work to your instructions, it could be great fun for them to make instruments together and then use them in music sessions. This will heighten their appreciation of music sessions and give them a sense of accomplishment in being able to use something they have made. If you work with groups who are not fully capable of making instruments because of physical problems or an inability to comprehend instructions, you may find that they too would benefit by watching you make the instruments and helping whenever possible. If there is a workshop or an occupational therapy unit in the vicinity they may like to become involved by arranging for the people who attend their sessions to make instruments for you. Also local schools may be interested as it could be a way of introducing their pupils to the handicapped pupils. Your pupils could play the new instruments for them and perhaps they could give a short concert for you. In this way both handicapped and non-handicapped pupils will have the opportunity to meet, share music and be mutually helpful.

4: ENJOYMENT ONE-TO-ONE

There is something very special about music shared by two people. It can become an intimate experience that develops relationships between parent and child or teacher and pupil. It can aid in understanding your child to a degree that you had perhaps not imagined possible, particularly if he has little or no speech. You are sharing with him something that he feels and enjoys as much as you do and that he does not need intellectual power to appreciate. Through this common interest you can gain an insight into his world and lead him into a broader experience of life.

There are both advantages and disadvantages in sharing music one-to-one. The main disadvantage is that there is no one else to work with should a session stagnate for any reason. If you are working with a group and one person is unresponsive, you can work with the other pupils and return to him once in a while to try to gain a response. In a one-to-one situation your unresponsive child is the only person with whom to work. If in a group one person is disruptive he can be ignored or removed from the group. Your disruptive child is with you and you must cope. If one person in a group chooses to follow another activity during part of a session, such as looking out of the window or reading a book, the music can continue without his aid. Lose your child's attention in a one-to-one session and there is no session. You will need even more patience at times when sharing music one-to-one. But please, try not to become discouraged. You may have to persevere and be prepared to wait weeks or many months before you see tangible results – but they will be all the more welcome when they finally appear.

Another disadvantage is that your child will have no one with whom to compare his progress. If he is mentally very able he may be satisfied with his progress and become lazy about attempting more demanding things. If he is working with a

group he will try harder to improve his performance ii
keep up with or ahead of his fellow pupils.

Reasons for individual sessions
For a number of reasons, not all your pupils will be able to
cope with music sessions in the company of others. Some may
be overactive to the extent that they disrupt the session by
pacing or running up and down and distracting everyone's
attention. They are not learning anything during sessions and
are preventing their fellow pupils from enjoying a profitable
time.

Perhaps some have habits that are not easily controlled while
they are within a group. They may be aggressive towards fellow
pupils, attempting to scratch, bite or kick them, or may even be
over-affectionate, hugging and kissing those sitting near.

If some have autistic characteristics it may be too difficult to
develop a programme which caters for them in a group
situation.

Those who are excessively shy or timid of others may retreat
from the group.

If you have pupils who are too severely physically handicapped it may be inadvisable under certain circumstances for
you to take them into a group because of a risk of infection by
other pupils' coughs and colds or because they are not well
enough to be moved to the place where the group meets.

Some pupils are relatively too intelligent to fit into the
groups you have. They may be very keen to learn to play an
instrument or to learn to read music.

It may be that some pupils cannot cope initially in a group
and need one-to-one work until they can be integrated into a
suitable group at a later date.

You may need to withdraw a pupil from a group for one-to-
one work for a limited period if he needs special attention to
develop a skill, is being disruptive or you think he would
benefit more from individual attention.

Perhaps the best reason for your being alone with one pupil
is when you are the pupil's parent and you are spending a
happy time together sharing the experience of music.

Music activities
What are the kinds of activities that you can share with your child?

Singing
You don't have to sing like an operatic artiste in order to sing to your child. Most people have quite an acceptable singing voice. If you are someone who only sings in the bath, try singing to your child as well. You will probably find that despite your reluctance to give public performances you have an admiring audience in your child. If you have a genuine reason for not singing, such as an inability to recognise rise and fall in pitch, then use a tape or record of suitable songs and sit with your child listening to the music and encouraging him to sing the songs. Emphasize the words to him by speaking

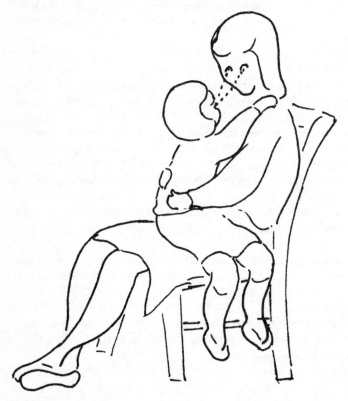

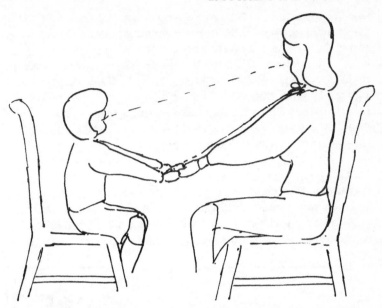

them whilst they are sung and by repeating the words to him afterwards. It could be that by concentrated effort you will improve your pitch and actually be able to follow the melody. My son John claims to be tone deaf, but over the years has succeeded in whistling 'God save the Queen' and 'Onward Christian Soldiers' well enough for us to recognise which one he is attempting!

There is a very soothing element in being sung to by another person. Your child might not appear to be aware of what you are singing if he is severely handicapped, yet it is usual for a mother to sing lullabies to a tiny baby who has extremely limited understanding of what the song is about. A baby appreciates the combination of rhythm, melody and security at these times. If your child is small enough to hold in your arms, sing to him in this position. If he is bigger, sit him on your knee or sit facing him so that he can see that you are singing and you can make eye contact with him.

Development of speech through song
If your child does not speak, only makes sounds, has indistinct speech or a stammer, or finds it difficult to put thoughts into

words, you can help him by singing songs with him. By using songs which he responds to, or by singing question and answer songs, he will be drawn into a situation where he wants to use words. There are well known children's songs which involve making sounds of various kinds, such as 'Old MacDonald's Farm'. If your child is older or is a mentally or physically handicapped adult who requires an adult outlook on life, write your own songs for him or adapt songs that he enjoys (see Chapter Seven, Let's Write Songs).

Listening together

Introduce your child to as wide a variety of sounds and music as you can. Think how many different kinds of sounds there are and how vast is the variety of music available. Sound tapes and cards are available for use with your child. He can listen to the

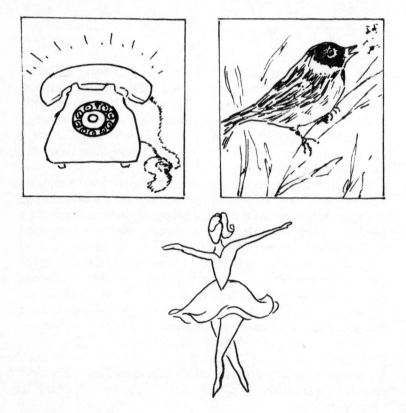

sound and choose the picture of the object that makes that sound. For example: the sound of a telephone ringing to match a picture of a telephone; a bird song to match with a picture of birds. You could quite easily make up your own set using familiar sounds in your child's environment. Some sounds are more obviously musical than others but all of them can be helpful in your child's perception of the world around him.

Introduce him to many different types of music. It is not necessary to own a large number of records or tapes as you can join a lending library. The regular favourites could then be purchased to form your own collection. Listen to ballet music and show your child pictures or drawings of a ballerina; play waltzes to him and show him pictures of couples dancing; tell him about other countries and introduce him to their costumes and folk music; show him pictures of different instruments and play him examples of each. For example: bagpipes, violin, trumpet, piano, alpine horn and so on. Divide them into groups according to whether they are blown, bowed or struck. How far this can develop will depend on your child's mental ability. However just sitting together and enjoying a variety of musical sounds, however limited his ability, is time well spent. Perhaps later you will be able to extend this activity to actually attending some concerts and seeing and hearing live music.

Motivation
Many of the mentally handicapped people I meet are not motivated to do anything without physical or verbal prompting and this also applies to some physically handicapped people. Some find the mental process required to do anything too great, or else lack the necessary mental ability, while others find the physical effort needed is daunting. Songs sung to your child about activities can lead him into action in a pleasant way. For example: songs about walking, washing, cleaning teeth, brushing hair and so on. When the activity is preceded or accompanied by a song which is fun for him, he will be more likely to do what is required without objection.

The pleasing sound made by an instrument will motivate your child to touch, shake, strike, beat or blow it. Have a small collection of instruments for his use and introduce him to the way in which they make sounds. If he has a physical problem,

CLEANING YOUR TEETH
by Sarah Applin & Sally-Ann Jolliffe
Lower Sixth 'A' Level Students

Pick up the brush,   take off the cap,

squeeze the   tube   and   turn   on   the   tap.

8va

Put   on   the   paste,   not   on   your   face,

now clean your teeth with not too much haste.

Round and round, up and down,

front and back, mind your tongue.

encourage him to use his weaker hand or arm by placing the instrument nearer to the side you want him to use. Some instruments can be adapted to be played with the feet if hands or arms are not strong enough. There are specially produced electronic instruments on the market for use by handicapped people. An example is the 'Touch-a-Tune' (see Useful Addresses, page 191). It consists of a flat key-board with notes which are wide, well spaced and each a different colour. It can be played with fingers, hands, arms, feet or even the head. A sensitivity control makes it attractive to those who are unable to put pressure onto the notes and it has a volume control. It also has a socket for head phones to enable the hearing impaired to use it. Each note has its own switch at the rear of the instrument. It can be used on a table or on the floor or can be secured to a surface. Its appealing appearance invites attempts to play it. A parent or teacher can invent many different activities using it. For instance, a colour code can be made up so that your child can learn to play tunes on it; a game to find the note which will play can encourage your child to reach out and move from note to note; the letter names of each note of the scale (C,D,E,F,G,A,B) can be written on the corresponding notes of the instrument, so enabling him to play a tune by reading the letters.

'Touch-a-Tune'

Music has power to motivate movement. It is very difficult to sit still when a military band plays a stirring march. Utilize this power by choosing music for your child to help him to move in the way you see he needs most.

Perhaps your child is very withdrawn and does not attempt to move on his own, or is physically handicapped and finds the effort too great to want to move. There are many attractive musical boxes on the market that are made in different shapes. They are operated by pulling a handle suspended on a string. Hang one of these within reach of your child and activate it for him. Then aid him to use it himself. See if he will then attempt to do it by himself. As he learns to make it play, hang it further and further from him so that he will need to make more effort to reach and operate it. You could use sleigh bells in a similar way or make up a series of instruments hung on a bar which attract his attention and invite him to play them. A sound mat to roll on is also available from the makers of the 'Touch-a-Tune'.

If he cannot walk by himself, your child will enjoy walking or marching to music with your help. Various types of movement exercises are more meaningful when performed to a musical accompaniment that matches the activity. Play games with your child using music that varies in tempo. Walk or run to the faster sections and walk slowly or crawl when the music slows. As your child becomes used to this game, allow him to follow the directions that the music gives. Select various kinds of music to suggest different movements, for instance, hopping jumping or skipping. These games can be enjoyed by children with only a little ability to move, right through to the most able, simply by adapting the movements according to ability. Children confined to a wheelchair can be involved by your wheeling them or by wheeling themselves around to the music, or by being gently swung between two people if they are not too delicate or too heavy to lift.

Exercises for those in wheelchairs

It is possible to exercise most parts of the body while sitting in a wheelchair. Sing songs to your child to encourage him to raise his arms separately, then together, his legs and his head, to bend forward or to one side.

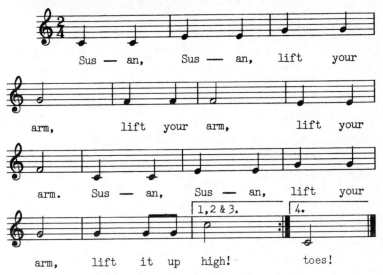

Susan, Susan, lift your arm, lift your arm, lift your arm. Susan, Susan, lift your arm, lift it up high! toes!

Extra verses to this song can be written, such as:

> Susan, Susan, kick your leg (or legs)
> Kick your leg, kick your leg,
> Susan, Susan, kick your leg,
> Kick it up high.

> . . . lift your head,
> Look to the sky.

> . . . touch your toes,
> Bend to your toes.

Out of a wheelchair there are other exercises you can do with your child. Before attempting these, I would strongly advise you to make certain that they are suitable for your particular child by first consulting his doctor or physiotherapist and showing what you intend to do. It is possible that they could be harmful in certain cases, so do check first to make absolutely sure that they are correct for your child.

Remember that when you are handling or moving your child you are expressing your feelings for him. He can tell by the way you move him what you think of him and you can convey your love for him through touch. It is useful to try these exercises on a friend first, and to ask your friend to do them to you, so that you can feel what it is like to be moved in this way.

Legs

Place your child on a comfortable mat and hold one of his legs gently at the ankle. Bend his knee then straighten his leg again. Repeat this with the other leg or both legs together. Do this in time to gently swaying music played live, or to specially chosen recorded music.

Hips

After a few minutes change to the next exercise. This time hold both his ankles and raise and bring first his right leg over his left

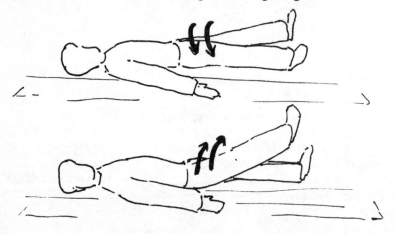

and then his left leg over his right, thus obtaining movement of his hips.

This part of his body receives little exercise while he is sitting in a wheelchair. If your child's legs are drawn up, exercise his hips by holding him gently at the knees and rocking them from side to side to obtain movement of the hips. Accompany this by music of a tempo similar to that used for the first exercise.

Rolling
Lay your child flat on the mat and gently roll him over, first on to one side and then on to the other. Encourage him to help or to roll himself from his side to flat on his back. If he is able, teach him to roll over and over. Use your imagination in finding music to accompany this exercise, perhaps choosing a drum roll, harp music or even a song about acrobats.

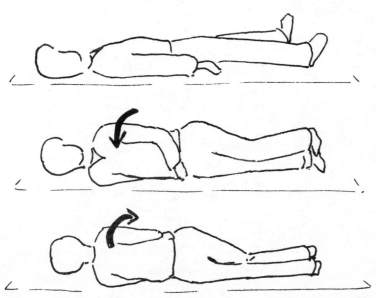

Fingers and hands

Exercise his hands by bending and straightening his fingers and rotating his wrists. Choose music which you think matches the movements you are making and which helps you to do them, as well as making it an enjoyable activity for him.

Arms

Exercise his arms, bending and stretching them from the elbow and moving them at the shoulder. If he has a certain amount of use of his arms, use fairly lively music to encourage him to move them around or to pull on your arms.

Lying and sitting

For this exercise choose music that has a rise and fall in its melody. Hold your child by his hands or at his wrists and raise him into a sitting position, then lower him back on to the mat. Alternatively hold his right or left hand with yours and raise him into a sitting position. In this way he will learn to use his

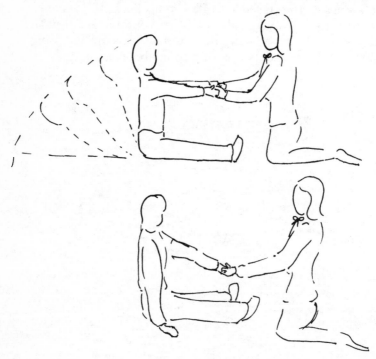

free hand to help himself to sit up and to balance. If your child is heavy you may find it easier to sit behind him and raise him into a sitting position by holding him at the shoulders. Again, encourage him to use his hands and arms to help raise and support himself.

Relaxation
End the session by relaxation. Sit with your legs either side of his legs, his body and head resting on you and your arms around him. While listening to quiet relaxing music, sway from side to side and hum or sing to him with the music.

Choose music to accompany these exercises very carefully. Think of what you are aiming at accomplishing and let the music add meaning to the exercises. This will help your child to relax and encourage him to participate rather than remain passive.

Music through the day
Specially chosen music to mark events through the day can make activities special and aid in their accomplishment.

Waking up
Do you like being woken up by an ear splitting bell of an alarm clock, by being called loudly, or by a bright light shining in your eyes? Wouldn't it be preferable to waken slowly to the sound of soft music? If you decide to try this with your child, do not choose music that is too lively first thing in the morning. Start the day in a gentle manner.

As a reward
If your child shows a preference for a particular piece of music, take advantage of this to encourage him to perform various tasks. Use music to reward him at the end of a task instead of using sweets (the dentist will be pleased!). For example, you are teaching him to dress himself. Perhaps he is learning to put on one item of clothing, or he may be able to dress completely but need to learn to put the clothes on in the correct order. Praise him when the task is completed correctly and reward him by letting him listen to a favourite song or piece of music, sung or played by you, or else recorded.

Listening tapes
There are times in the day when you wish to occupy your child while you are otherwise engaged. Make a tape for him for these occasions. Fill it with a variety of music, sounds and, if he enjoys stories, add these in between the music. If you read and record these yourself he will enjoy them even more, as your voice will be speaking to him while you cannot be right beside him. You will also be able to match the length of the stories to his concentration span and tell them at a speed that you know will make it easy for him to understand. Likewise songs sung by you on tape will have more appeal.

Anticipation
If we plan a holiday or an outing for ourselves, much of the enjoyment is found in laying the plans and thinking of what it

will be like, finding out information and building up a picture ahead of the event. We often forget the need for this anticipation when we plan activities for our handicapped child or pupil. Too often we have everything planned to the last detail, dress him up and set off, without thinking of building up for him a picture of where he is going and what will happen when he arrives. One way this can be done is by singing songs about a forthcoming event. For example, if you are planning a bus ride sing the well known children's song 'The wheels on the bus' ahead of the event and, if possible, when you see the bus show him the wheels, the windscreen wipers and listen to the horn and the bell. If a suitable song is not available, make up a song which describes what you will be doing. Making up your own songs is not as difficult as you might think (see Chapter Seven, Let's Write Songs). The songs can then be sung after the event to recall the experiences enjoyed. Perhaps you can add another song about anything that went wrong, such as losing the way or a downpour of rain.

Bedtime
When bedtime is drawing near, how about bringing your child's day to a close with music that will calm him and then music that will send him to sleep? As you begin the bedtime routine, play taped music of his favourite songs, with the lively ones first, gradually slowing the pace towards bedtime. Some of my own most treasured memories are of my mother playing a beautiful piece of music on the piano when I had gone to bed. She would sometimes practise the piano for a while at my bedtime. I would then ask her to play that particular piece last and remind her not to speak when she finished it. It created such a beautiful relaxed feeling in me that I did not want the spell broken by words. Could you create such an atmosphere for your child so that he is relaxed and drifts off to sleep?

A time for silence
When planning to use music in your child's day remember that music times will make more impact if they follow times when no music is played. Music all day long can become very tiring, over stimulating, or become like wallpaper – not noticed after its initial attractiveness has been admired. Quiet times when no

music is played are important. Too much of even the best things in life can be bad.

Learning to read and play music

Does your child show ability to play music? Is he eager to learn to play an instrument, or do you think that he is capable of learning? Some blind people show ability to play music by ear. This is probably because they rely so much on listening and develop this sense more in place of seeing. Some sighted people also have a good ear for music. If your child has the ability to play music by ear it is possibly best to encourage him to develop this rather than endeavour to teach him music in a more formal way which he may find difficult. It will just depend on your child, what his handicaps are and how well he can learn something new. Some handicapped people have far more ability to appreciate and play music than would be expected from observing other aspects of their lives.

If you wish your child to learn to play an instrument, find a good teacher who has had experience in teaching pupils with learning difficulties or a physical handicap, or who is able to adapt her methods sufficiently to understand your child's needs. If you cannot find someone like this, then use whatever ability you have to teach him yourself, or begin by learning an instrument and use the knowledge you gain to teach him. Sometimes, however, it is easier for a stranger to teach your child as he may sit and listen better to a less familiar person. Whoever is teaching him, he will probably need regular lessons of short duration.

One of my former pupils is a mentally handicapped disturbed adolescent. He was keen to play tunes on a xylophone using the letter names of the notes. I wrote the tunes out for him using the letters only and he played the corresponding letters marked on the xylophone. Music activities held his concentration, whereas at other times it was extremely difficult to keep him occupied for more than a few minutes.

Another young man readily learned to play scales and arpeggios, thus helping him to use all his fingers rather than just the two he normally used to pick out melodies on the piano. He is a very withdrawn young man, not wishing to communicate with anyone and having strange mannerisms. His musical ability aided him in forming relationships. He learned to play the xylophone in time to a piano accompaniment and to choose the pieces he wished to play. From the arpeggios he began to develop chords and to harmonise using both hands. Music to him is a life line between his enclosed world and the rest of humanity. He and I were able to build up a very special relationship and understanding which led to his learning sign language. He had ceased to speak, apart from the odd word or two to his mother, and had only spoken a few phrases as a child. Through signing he was able to sign answers to questions addressed to him. Relationships built up in this way need cultivating so that the person's full potential can be reached. It is not usually wise to expect the person to be able to relate in the same way to another teacher. He will need long and careful teaching and a gradual widening of confidence in order to include other people. If another teacher uses the same methods she will still need to build up a relationship, as did the first teacher. A second teacher may even be viewed with disdain and the pupil may need to keep his relationship with the other teacher as a bridge to other people. He may feel abandoned if that vital link is broken for any reason.

Improvisation
This is the use of any instrument (or the voice) to produce music which is composed as it is played. It can be very effective in a one-to-one situation. You may find that it is easiest for your child to use a drum and for you to play the piano. It is

possible to do this regardless of whether you have had any formal training in playing the piano (as we discovered in Chapter One). Encourage your child to beat the drum. If he is very severely mentally or physically handicapped it may take many patient months of work to enable him to begin to do this. For example, I have one pupil who would not hold a drum stick – her hand automatically released its grip after she had grasped it initially. She was also given items to grip by another teacher: brightly coloured bricks, soft coloured toys and plastic 'squeezy' shapes. A third teacher helped her to feed herself with a spoon. I recently rearranged the position of the drum for her. I put it on a table beside her and rested her wrist on the edge of the drum at shoulder height. In this unusual position she grasped and held the drum stick and began to beat varied rhythms to my accompaniment. She now looks at me and smiles when I sing her name while she is beating the drum, and at her most recent session she gently put the drum stick down on the drum when I ceased to play and beamed a smile as I moved forward to congratulate her on her performance. Each teacher has been able to help the other and each activity has helped the other towards success.

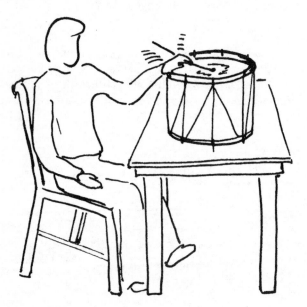

Play games with your child. If he stops beating the drum, you stop playing the piano. When he restarts, you restart. Stop while he is beating and see how he reacts. Vary your rhythm and see if he copies. Play loudly, play softly and watch his response. Depending on his ability he may respond immediately or it may take weeks or months for him to get the feel of what you are both doing. The exercise can be very satisfying for both of you. If you feel a oneness and exhilaration after playing a piece together don't forget to tell him how much you have enjoyed it and thank him for it. Do this whether or not you think he understands everything you say. If he is able to express himself, give him the opportunity to tell you what the experience means to him. Always tell him how pleased you are if he has put effort into the activity, even if the results are not exciting. I have had excellent results using this method with mentally handicapped people ranging in ability from severely to mildly handicapped. The experience is something which grows and develops confidence and awareness.

'Conversation' on a drum

Another way of using a drum with your child is to beat a message to him on a drum which is placed between you. Encourage him to beat back a reply to you. Beat together and lead him to change rhythm or follow his beat as he changes the rhythm. You may find this easier to do at first if you are a little apprehensive at the thought of using a piano.

Strumming a guitar

Sit with your child facing you and encourage him to strum the strings of a guitar. The shape and sound of the guitar is very attractive to even the least able child. Sing to him and change the chords while he strums the guitar, thus producing the sound for himself. He will feel very involved in the music making if he is able to learn to take part in this way.

If you are really enjoying music yourself and are prepared to share yourself as well as the music with your child or pupil, you are bound to succeed. Progress will vary with different pupils but the joy that both you and they feel can be experienced whether a pupil had learnt to sing a whole song or whether he has just held a drum stick for the first time and tapped on the drum. Always be positive and optimistic in your outlook and recognise success in the little steps along the way.

5: GROUP MUSIC MAKING

As a teacher you will probably have groups of various sizes more often than one pupil at a time. Purely from an economic point of view it makes sense to deal with groups rather than on a one-to-one basis, however advantageous it may be to your pupils' progress to have individual sessions. How many pupils are included in a group may depend on you or may be someone else's choice. It is far better if you can choose the size of groups yourself and decide which pupils will attend rather than have large numbers thrust willy-nilly into music, making it almost impossible to have constructive sessions. There is nothing more frustrating for pupils and teacher than to have a potentially enjoyable and well planned session ruined by too many people being together, or by a difficult combination of people who do not form a group easily. Once groups are formed they should not be invaded by extras or individual pupils swapped from group to group for no real reason, as this will break down the group identity which can be formed even between very severely mentally handicapped people. Pupils who are added to or subtracted from music groups like counters on a board for reasons such as, 'John's been to music a few times and likes it, so we thought that we'd send Robert to have a go now,' will not progress. Any benefits they have gained will be lost and they will become confused or disillusioned by the sudden changes made for no apparent or carefully planned reason.

Seating
You will need to consider the best seating arrangement for pupils so that they are comfortably placed in order to participate.

Small groups
If you choose to have between four and eight pupils in a group

you will need them to sit where you can see each person and have a full view of each face. This can be accomplished by forming a semi-circle. If you are playing a piano you will need to have it in a position where you can play it and still be in close contact with your pupils. Ask any helpers to sit between pupils. They can aid them to participate (although you will need to ensure that the helpers are not doing the work for them) and they will be able to concentrate on the pupils rather than talking to each other. If your pupils tend to wander around rather than sit on chairs, it may be best to sit them around a table but still in a semi-circle so that they can see you. Groups made up of pupils who are able to play pitched instruments may find it easier to sit at individual tables or together with others in the group who are playing similar instruments.

Larger groups
How you place pupils in larger groups will depend upon the nature of the activity. It is usually best to form a circle so that everyone can see what is happening. If your pupils do not need constant surveillance or do not lose concentration rapidly, you may find it better for them to sit in rows.

Let's enjoy ourselves
Now is the time to use your enthusiasm. The moment your pupils enter the room they must sense your pleasure at having their company and your eagerness to share music with them. An atmosphere of happiness is felt and does not always need words to express it. They will be eager to come to music and will learn to anticipate the joy of a shared experience. Of course there will be times when both you and they will feel 'off colour' and it will be necessary to work at a lower pitch, but the atmosphere created by previous sessions will tide you over these less positive times.

An assistant who is as enthusiastic as you are is a treasure worth guarding. A rapport can be built up between the two of you and you can take it in turns to lead or assist each other, especially if your assistant has developed her musical ability too. When one or the other is absent, the pupils will not miss sessions as it will be possible to maintain continuity with one of you carrying on the programme.

It is particularly helpful when working with pupils who have little or no speech or singing ability to have an assistant who can add to the volume of your singing and who can reply to questions on the pupils' behalf. For example, you sing a song which asks 'How are you?' A pupil smiles and looks happy in reply and your assistant says, 'Tim's happy today, aren't you, Tim?' Robert looks miserable, so she says, 'Oh, Robert's not happy. What's the matter, Robert?' You perhaps add, 'He wants to go back to bed.' Your assistant looks at him and says, 'No he doesn't, do you, Robert?' By this time Robert is probably laughing at the conversation on his behalf and is ready to participate fully in the session.

A sense of understanding between you and an assistant can add tremendously to the enjoyment and usefulness of sessions. It will not always be necessary to work out details in advance, but both of you will be in tune with each other's needs and the desire of your pupils. If such an assistant leaves it can be very difficult to find a suitable replacement. Ideally a new assistant should participate in sessions for a while, before the other leaves, in order to observe the programme and learn to participate in it in a similar way.

What shall we do?
There are different kinds of musical activities which you can share with your pupils, depending on their ability and willingness to co-operate.

General music group
This is most suitable for a small group of pupils (up to eight preferably) and it includes singing and the use of instruments. Young physically handicapped and moderately or severely mentally handicapped people of all ages will find this type of session useful and enjoyable. It can be easily adjusted to suit pupils of varying ability and can form a programme which aids each pupil to develop systematically, as well as gaining benefit from working in a group situation. The songs used in this session, apart from 'Shake the Bells' and 'Beat the Drum' (see 3. and 4. below), are taken from *The First Book of Children's Play Songs* and *The Second Book of Children's Play Songs* by P. Nordoff and C. Robbins (see Reading List, page 187).

1. Anticipation song – 'Something is Going to Happen'
Begin the programme in a definite way. A song such as this informs your pupils that the music session has begun and that a happy time is in store.

2. Welcome or rollcall song – 'The Rollcall Song'
Use the names of the pupils in the group. Your pupil's name is for him the most important thing that he hears. Look at each pupil as you sing his name, shake hands with him (or arrange for your assistant or other helpers to do so) or call each pupil out in turn to stand near you while you sing, then shake hands at the end of the verse. If you have pupils who are able to sing or to say some of the words of the song, let them play an active part by singing the words with you or shaking hands with the person named. Speak or sing the greeting 'Hello' again at the end of each verse to give each pupil the opportunity to respond verbally, whether or not you think he is capable of doing so. A song which has a very definite reply, such as 'Here I am', can encourage a sung or spoken reply. If the song is sung pretending that you do not know where the pupil is, it will encourage others to identify him for you or for him to identify himself. This type of song provides scope for work with the least able who can only sit and listen, look or wave a hand, right up to those who are able to sing both question and answer and identify each other correctly.

3. Group activity – 'Shake the Bells'
It is good to involve all the group in an activity. If they are able to use instruments it will be easier to involve each pupil in a combined activity, but if their ability is limited, shaking bells is one of the simplest activities. All the pupils are given sleigh bells to hold. The first verse could be a general verse. In subsequent verses name one person per verse. Encourage the other pupils to listen and watch the pupil whose name is being sung while they remain silent. If practical, call each pupil to stand in front of the group for his own verse. End by singing everyone's name:

> Tina, George and Willi shake the bells,
> Roddy, Sheila, shake the bells.
> Margaret, Tony, shake the bells,
> Shake, shake, shake the bells.

SHAKE THE BELLS

Key of: G Major

Shake, shake, shake, shake, shake the

bells. Shake, shake, shake, the bells.

Pe — ter Will — iams shake the bells.

Shake, shake, shake the bells. Shake, shake,

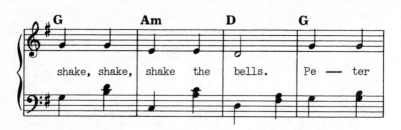

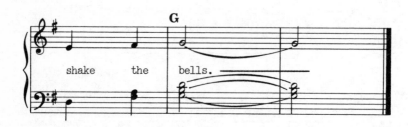

Rosie is severely mentally and physically handicapped. One of the highlights of her week is this activity. She becomes very excited when the bells come into sight. She is able to hold them in her right hand (she cannot use her left hand or arm or her legs). She laughs and shakes the bells with vigour.

4. Drumming – piano and individual drum improvisation
Call or bring pupils one at a time to sit by the drum near the piano so that both you and the other pupils can see what is happening. Play to the pupil and encourage him to beat the drum (see Improvisation, page 65). You can sing as well (see 'Beat the Drum', page 105), adding phrases as you sing. Rosie, who enjoys shaking the bells, has also developed the ability to beat the drum. Her wild beating of the drum is now becoming more subdued and she alternates between loud and soft. This exercise is a wonderful outlet for her as it is the only way she can express herself and make a noise which is positive.

Terry is less severely mentally and physically handicapped. He can speak and is able to walk with a fair degree of success, although he falls over frequently and bumps into people and objects. He makes beating the drum into a game which involves other group members. I play some chords on the piano and he beats the drum. When he pauses I cease to play. He begins to beat and I accompany him. This is repeated with pauses of varying length determined by him. The rest of the group become very involved, almost holding their breath during the pauses and willing him with their eyes and by soft whispers to beat the drum, so that I will play and the music continue.

Over the years I have found the use of the drum very effective with my pupils. They enjoy the sound made by it and become involved in the rhythm. It is a non-verbal expression between us and even very severely mentally handicapped pupils enjoy watching a fellow pupil taking his turn. The use of the drum aids manual dexterity, builds confidence, develops expression, brings recognition of the rhythm of words and can be used to make non-verbal conversation, as well as being great fun for everyone involved. Do not expect to see the results immediately. Sometimes it is necessary to teach your pupil to hold the drum stick first (which may take hours or months). Others who can beat the drum without difficulty may take weeks, months or in some cases years to really gain full benefit from the activity. For example, some pupils may at first beat the drum repetitively with no break or rhythm pattern and regardless of what is played on the piano. This is of little benefit as they are still within themselves and not aware of what is happening. Sometimes it is necessary physically to prompt a pupil to beat while you count 'One – two –', then raise his arm in order to create a pause.

Angus, who is severely mentally handicapped and without speech, took several years to gain sufficient confidence to be able to participate in improvisation. He was an extremely shy young man who retreated from anyone who approached him. I tried through music to build up his confidence. It took many months of work at a basic level (singing to him, encouraging him to shake hands with me, gradually moving closer to him until he allowed me to sit right beside him) to bring him to the point where he was ready and willing to use instruments and become an active member of his group. He began to beat on the drum but had no idea of rhythm and needed a verbal prompt to continue for more than a few seconds. I began beating the drum too, counting then raising my arm. He copied this and was able to beat in twos, threes and fours. Then I began to sing to him while we both beat the rhythm of 'Angus knows how to beat that drum.' Over a number of weeks he developed a degree of accuracy in this, so I then tried playing the piano accompaniment. He beat the rhythm perfectly and showed pleasure in my praise of his accomplishment. I am now leading him to follow other rhythm patterns and guiding him to cope with unexpected changes of rhythm. Angus is less shy than he was and is willing to make relationships with people other than myself. By learning to cope first with the predictable and now the unpredictable in music he is learning to cope with similar situations in his daily life.

5. Listening to music – live or recorded instruments
I often include recorded music in a group session and note the reaction of each person, thereby learning what style of music they enjoy or whether they are aware of different kinds of music. I deal with this aspect in greater detail in Chapter Six, Listening to Music.

6. Goodbye song – 'Goodbye'
It is pleasant to end a session in a definite manner rather than let it peter out. Again names can be sung which provide a sense of security and importance for each pupil.

Singing group or choir
Some people enjoy the sound of their own voice while others are reluctant to make themselves heard. A singing group can be a platform for the bold pupils and an aid for the shy ones or those who have problems in producing sounds. A group of pupils can enjoy singing favourite songs and, as everyone is involved, there is no one to stand around criticising the quality of the sound produced. Pupils usually enjoy songs with a chorus, so that even if they cannot remember all the verses there can be full participation when the chorus is repeated.

Often a pupil will volunteer to sing a solo. Allow time towards the end of the session for anyone who may wish to give a solo performance and make this aspect part of the group session. As pupils gain confidence through singing in a group, even the shy ones may want to sing a solo occasionally. Appreciation by the group encourages the pupil to volunteer again and his tone, volume and enunciation will improve at each attempt.

A singing group is an informal and happy time spent together sharing songs that are chosen by the group members or introduced by the leader. Singing around the piano at home is a pastime that almost died out with the arrival of television. For handicapped people its revival can bring warmth and a feeling of belonging to people who need it as much as, and maybe more than, those who are able in body and mind.

A choir is a singing group of a more formal or sophisticated nature. Its members sing together because it is a pleasure to do so, but there is more formality in that pieces of music are being learnt and there may be parts to practise, if the pupils are capable of learning them. Members of the choir may be chosen from the singing group because they are prepared to put effort into this kind of activity. When forming a choir of handicapped people the emphasis is usually on benefit for the individual and enjoyment derived from a group activity, rather than on perfection in the end result. Of course, what is produced may also make very pleasant listening, despite the fact that the choir members are chosen not only for their ability to sing and quality of voice but because of their need to be involved in this kind of group activity. A choir demands more of its members – discipline, work, co-operation and a certain amount of dedication. Also, the ultimate aim of a choir is to perform so that others may enjoy what they have prepared. Performance is an extremely important aspect, particularly for pupils who are not easily able to produce something for other people to admire.

Percussion groups

If your pupils are able to participate in activities fairly readily (are able to hold beaters and drum sticks or can learn to repeat a pattern of notes on a xylophone or rhythm on a drum, or can follow instruction to shake bells at the correct time) you can have an interesting time together learning to combine sounds or to accompany a melody played on an instrument. For example, Philip, a very withdrawn young man, able bodied but without speech, could pick out melodies on a chord organ and learned to use the chord buttons to provide the bass. He led the group of less able pupils while they accompanied him on percussion instruments. Their ability was limited to playing when he began to play and stopping when he stopped (this had to be taught to some of the group). Another group consisted of pupils able to beat a rhythmic pattern on a drum, repeat a pattern of notes on a xylophone, play the cymbal or triangle and shake bells. They were able to provide an interesting and varied accompaniment as directed by the teacher, or by using their own imagination and feel for the music.

It can be interesting to write out music for such groups using symbols and colours to represent the sounds made by various instruments and the length of sound required. Your pupils may be able to help you in deciding which symbols to choose and how to write them out, thus making an active contribution to the creation of a piece of music.

Here are a few examples:

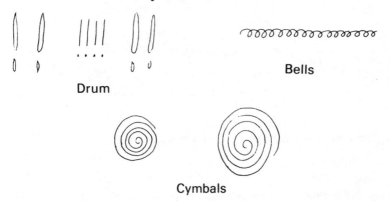

Drum

Bells

Cymbals

Music activity for a large group
You may have a large group of pupils (perhaps up to thirty) and want to involve them in an activity using music. You could use movement and music (see Chapter Eight, Music to Move) or you could sit with the pupils in a circle around you and involve everyone in activities one at a time or as a group. You will need more helpers according to the severity of handicap. Begin with a cheerful song of welcome, perhaps naming some or all of the pupils. Use action songs with helpers aiding pupils to perform them if necessary (such as 'If you're happy and you know it, clap your hands', etc.). Take pupils, one at a time, to the centre of the circle and show the rest of the group the pupil's new dress, hairstyle, or identify the colour of shoes or clothing. Allow the pupil to bring possessions to show the group, such as a photograph, a book or a soft toy (or whatever is appropriate

to their age and understanding). Sing about the pupil by name and about what she has to show, using a song you have made up (see Chapter Seven), or make up words and sing them to a familiar song, such as:

> Margaret has a new book,
> A new book, a new book,
> Margaret has a new book
> And here it is today.

(*Sung to the tune* 'Charlie is my darling')

or adapt a song to suit your needs, such as:

> There is a girl from Blackmoor
> From Blackmoor, from Blackmoor,
> There is a girl from Blackmoor,
> And her name is Cynthia Jones.
>
> And she has a pretty yellow dress,
> A yellow dress, a yellow dress,
> And she has a pretty yellow dress,
> And her name is Cynthia Jones.

(*Adapted from the song* 'Akin Drum')

Choose a song to sing and dance to with a pupil, inside or around the outside of the circle, such as, 'She'll be coming round the mountain when she comes' or, 'Skip to my lou'. With the former you can adapt verses: 'She'll be wearing a blue jacket when she comes . . .' or, 'She'll be riding in a carriage . . .' (for someone in a wheelchair), and with the latter you can use the chorus to dance to and adapt the verses to apply to individual pupils: 'Susan has her brown boots on . . .'

Music to aid communication
Perhaps you have pupils who are able to say only a few words, or whose speech is indistinct or nonexistent. You can design activities to aid them to communicate and to improve the ability that they have. Choose songs that require an answer such as:

> Tony Clark, Tony Clark, where are you?
> Here I am, here I am, how do you do?

(*Sung to the tune of* 'Finger family')

Encourage the pupil to reply, 'Here I am', or 'Here', or to make a sound in reply.

Write songs about the days of the week, the seasons or the weather conditions, which require a response or encourage discussion (see Chapter Seven). Sing songs about food and discuss the likes and dislikes of your pupils. For those in the group who cannot speak, or to encourage discussion with those who can, prepare pictures which relate to the subject in hand and allow the pupils to participate by choosing the appropriate picture or discussing it. For example, sing a song about going for a ride (see 'Here comes the bus', Chapter Seven) and talk about where they would like to go and what they would like to see. Have pictures to illustrate the places your pupils will be likely to choose (see Chapter Seven for suggested drawings).

Write songs about colour in order to teach the names of colours or to bring colour into discussion (for example, 'The colour is red' in Chapter Seven, or 'Who has a red shirt?' from *The First Book of Children's Play Songs* by P. Nordoff and C. Robbins).

Use or write your own counting songs (for example, 'The counting song' from the Nordoff and Robbins *Second Book of Children's Play Songs*) and encourage the pupils to count each other. If they have difficulty in doing this, move pupils one by one from one side of the room to the other, so that they can see what 'one' is or what 'six' means. If their ability is more advanced, make up songs about money and what they can buy with 'x' pennies or pounds.

These songs will become familiar to the pupils and will encourage them to learn things that they might otherwise find difficult or tedious. They will encourage the pupils to talk about the subject mentioned in the songs, thus increasing their understanding, vocabulary and ability to express themselves.

Music to teach specific ideas
The following lessons were prepared by Helen Newman as part of a curriculum pack for severely mentally handicapped children, aged between six and eight years of age, at an ESN(S) school. I am including the lessons on 'Falling', 'Going up and falling down' and 'Loud and quiet'. Other lessons in the pack included 'Hands and fingers', 'Water' and 'A day at the

seaside'. The three given below may aid you in preparing similar activities for your pupils. Helen Newman is a teacher (B. Ed. Honours in Mental Handicap) teaching 14–16 year old pupils in Hertfordshire.

FALLING

Overall aim
To direct the children's attention to the quality of 'falling'. 'Falling' is taken to mean a movement from 'high' to 'low' in a variety of different contexts. It is intended to give the children experience of a number of examples and to relate this to music.

Specific objectives
1.   Children to hear and produce 'falling' music.
2.   Children to make their own 'falling' body movements.
3.   Children to experience and produce combinations of 'falling' actions and 'falling' music.
4.   Children to sing a variety of songs with a 'falling' theme.

Situation
Children sitting around teacher, in a group.

Duration
Approximately 20 minutes.

Materials
Wooden xylophone
Drum/tambour
Paper – tissue/crêpe
Pennies
Leaves
'Michael Mouse'
Paper 'hill' and 'cheese'

OBJECTIVE	METHOD	CRITERIA OF SUCCESS
1. Children to watch falling tissue paper and listen to downward glissando.	Teacher drops a piece of tissue paper and plays a downward glissando on a wooden xylophone. Talks about 'falling'	Children to follow the tissue paper with their eyes.

	– how the music is falling; 'starting high – going down low'. Repeats dropping tissue paper.	
2. Children to make 'falling' arm movements.	Teacher shows children how to start with arms high and let them fall to sound of glissando. Children to repeat arm movements.	Children to initiate arm movements.
3. Children to watch 'falling' leaf.	Teacher talks to children about leaves falling from trees in Autumn. Blown from trees by wind. Has a leaf which children can watch falling 'high to low'.	Children to watch leaf falling.
4. Children to join in song 'Autumn Leaves' with hand action. (see Resources, page 84)	Teacher sings song about Autumn leaves falling. Encourages children to join in song with 'falling' hand actions – fluttering fingers from high to low on first 2 lines.	Children to attempt to join in song with hand actions.
5. Children to listen to leaves falling on drum.	Teacher drops a leaf on drum. Encourages children to be very quiet – can they hear it falling? Try pieces of paper and pennies. What is the difference? Short guessing game – close eyes and guess if teacher is dropping pennies or paper.	Children to look at object falling and talk about the sounds they make.

6. Children to listen to story of 'Humpty Dumpty' and join in with words and actions.	Teacher tells children the story of 'Humpty Dumpty' who 'falls' from a wall. Sings it through with 'falling' actions on 2nd line. Children to join in with song and actions.	Children to join in with song and try actions.
7. As objective 6, but with 'Jack and Jill'.	As method 6, but with 'Jack and Jill'. Have fingers walking up arm and falling down other side.	Children to join in with song and try actions.
8. Children to listen to the story of 'Michael Mouse' and accompany it with 'falling' music.	Teacher tells the story of 'Michael Mouse' – introduces him to the children and shows them how the 'glissando' on the xylophone makes the sound of his falling down the hill. Children to help accompany the story with the xylophone.	Children to make the sound of 'Michael Mouse' falling down the hill on xylophone.

RESOURCES

The Autumn Leaves
(Tune: 'Do you know the Muffin Man?')

1. The Autumn leaves have fallen down,
   Fallen down, fallen down.
   The Autumn leaves have fallen down,
   Fallen down.

2. The wind he came and blew them round,
   Blew them round, blew them round.
   The wind he came and blew them round,
   Blew them round.

(Adapted from 'This Little Puffin', E. Matterson, 1969).

Story of Michael Mouse
Green/brown cardboard hill – with piece of cheese at the top of the hill. Michael loves cheese and is desperate to get to the top of the hill. He tries climbing one side – nearly at top – falls down to bottom again (glissando) – tries other side – falls down to bottom again. Middle – falls down. Eventually – sadly walks around to the other side – there is a path! Walks up and eats the cheese!

GOING UP AND FALLING DOWN

Overall aim
To direct the children's attention to the qualities of 'falling down' and 'going up'. 'Going up' is taken to mean a movement from 'low' to 'high' in a variety of different contexts. The lesson is intended to complement the children's previous work on 'falling down'.

Specific objectives
1. Children to hear and produce music 'going up' and 'falling down'.
2. Children to experience physically 'going up' and 'falling down' movements.
3. Children to sing a variety of songs with a 'going up' and 'falling down' or 'coming down' theme.
4. Children to experience and produce combinations of 'going up' and 'falling down' actions and music.

Situation
Children sitting around teacher in a circle.

Duration
Approximately 20 minutes.

Materials
Balloon
Aeroplane
Xylophone
Michael Mouse
Cheese
Clock face
3 chime bars

OBJECTIVES	METHOD	CRITERIA OF SUCCESS
1. Children to recall aspects of 'falling' theme of previous lesson.	Teacher reminds children of previous lesson's 'falling down' theme. Asks children to show their arms 'falling down'. No prompts if possible. Sing 'Autumn Leaves' song with the children (see lesson one) with appropriate actions.	Children to show 'falling' arms action correctly and to join in with song and action.
2. Children to watch balloons 'going up' and 'falling down'.	Teacher reminds children of 'Jack and Jill' – 'going up' the hill then 'falling down'. Introduces idea of 'going up' then 'falling down'. Teacher blows up a balloon. Shows children how it is 'going up' and then 'falling down'. Lets children try throwing balloon into air.	Children to watch balloon going up and falling down and to throw balloons for themselves.
3. Children to watch aeroplane 'going up' and 'falling down' and to accompany movement with music.	Teacher shows children aeroplane 'going up' and 'falling down' – encourages children to make the movement and shows them how music on xylophone can accompany movement. Lets children make music and move aeroplane.	Children to make aeroplane go up and fall down and accompany movement with music.
4. Children to join in with 'The Grand Old Duke of York'.	Teacher introduces song about man who marches men up the	Children to join in with song.

	hill and then down again. Sings song through, then encourages children to join in.	
5. Children to join in 'Up I Stretch' song with appropriate actions (see Resources, page 88).	Teacher talks about 'stretching up' and 'bending down'. Shows children actions and then sings song with actions. Repeats, encouraging children to join in.	Children to join in with song and action.
6. Children to join in with 'Incy Wincy Spider' song.	Teacher goes through song with children, talking about 'going up' and 'falling down'. Sings song through and gets children to join in with actions.	Children to join in with song and actions.
7. Children to join in with 'Hickory Dickory Dock' and play chime bars to accompany song.	Teacher brings 'Michael Mouse' out for children. Talks about what happened to him in story. Encourages children to tell story of Michael climbing up clock to get cheese – frightened by clock striking 'one'. Gets children to sing song and play 3 chime bars – low, medium, high, in time with words 'Hickory Dickory Dock'. Discuss with children first, demonstrate and then practise. As children sing and 'play' song,	Children to talk about Michael and the cheese on the hill (see first lesson) and join in with music and song of 'Hickory Dickory Dock'.

teacher makes Mich-
ael run up her arm to
get cheese she holds
in her hand. Clock
face (paper) stuck on
hand with blu tak.

RESOURCES

Up I Stretch
Up I stretch on tippy toe,
Down to touch my heels I go.
Up again my arms I send,
Down again my knees I bend.

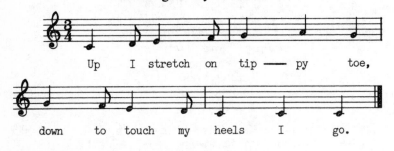

LOUD AND QUIET

Overall aim
To direct the children's attention to the qualities of 'loudness' and 'quietness'.

Specific objectives
1. Children to make a variety of 'loud' and 'quiet' sounds.
2. Children to talk about animals that make 'loud' and 'quiet' sounds.
3. Children to sing a variety of songs connected with the theme.

Situation
Children sitting around the teacher on small chairs. Floor space for instruments in centre.

Duration
20 to 30 minutes.

Materials
Drum
Tambourine
Wood beater
Michael Mouse
'Loud' objects – money, book, block.
'Quiet' objects – feather, string, paper.
Maracca

OBJECTIVES	METHOD	CRITERIA OF SUCCESS
1. Children to recall some of songs learnt in previous lessons.	Teacher asks children about songs they have learnt. 'Do you remember the song about the leaves?' Encourages children to sing and act with as little help as possible.	Children to recall some of newly learnt songs with actions.
2. Children to listen to a variety of objects falling and talk about noises made.	Teacher drops a variety of objects onto a drum and talks about loud/ quiet noises. Can the children guess what will be loud/quiet? Encourage language.	Children to listen to loud and quiet sounds.
3. Children to try making loud and quiet noises.	Teacher shows children how to clap very quietly and loudly. Shows how to tap drum very quietly and loudly. Encourages the children to make loud and quiet sounds.	Children to try making loud and quiet sounds.
4. Children to sing 'Ten fat sausages' and make sounds to accompany 'BANG'.	Teacher talks about the song – loud BANG and quieter pop – shows children how the BANG can	Children to sing and try to accompany it with sounds.

	be made with tambourine and 'pop' with wood beater. Sings song through showing children how to put in sounds. Encourage children to sing and play music for themselves.	
5. Children to talk about animals moving quietly/loudly.	Start with loud animals, elephants – try to make noise on tambourine – encourage children to try. Any other animals? Horse, hippo? Quiet animals, Michael Mouse, spider, snake – quiet sounds on tambourine.	Children to try quiet/loud sounds on tambourine.
6. Children to sing 'Three Blind Mice' and play accompanying sounds.	Mouse is quiet – talk about mice in 'Three Blind Mice' – what noise for cutting off tails? Show how to bang on tambourine for word 'cut'. Encourage children to sing song and play tambourine.	Children to sing song and play 'music' to accompany it.
7. Children to sing 'Incy Wincy Spider' with actions.	Talk about making fingers like a spider (which teacher had worked on in a lesson on 'Fingers and hands') and how spider is quiet. Encourage children to sing song and make correct finger actions.	Children to sing song and make appropriate actions.

8. Children to learn new song 'I Hear Thunder' and accompany song with sounds (see Resources, below).

Teacher talks about rain falling quietly – can the children think of a sound to make the rain (shake or tap tambourine)? Then thunder – loud bang – what could make this noise? Encourage children to find suitable noise. Talk about the song 'I Hear Thunder'. Sing song through – show children how to make bang for thunder on words 'thunder' and 'you'. Then rain for last two lines. Encourage all children to try to sing and do actions.

Children to sing new song with correct sounds.

RESOURCES

I Hear Thunder
(Tune: 'Frère Jacques')

I hear thunder,
I hear thunder.
Hark, don't you?
Hark, don't you?
Pitter-patter raindrops,
Pitter-patter raindrops,
I'm soaked through.
So are you!

Ability of pupils

The type of music activity that you will plan for your pupils will depend to a great degree upon their ability. Many physically handicapped pupils will be able to study music and learn to play instruments – but consideration of this aspect is beyond the scope of this particular book. Some of the activities described in this book you may find useful for young physically handicapped pupils. Their mental ability may compare with that of their able bodied friends. They may have less experience of life through an inability to explore for themselves, or their handicap may mean that they are immature for their age or have emotional problems. They may be behind with their education because of schooling lost through operations or medical appointments. You may wish to share music with children or adults who are so severely physically handicapped that it is difficult to tell the level of their understanding. Under these circumstances it is important for them that you find out as much as is known about their ability from other people and that you watch them for clues to their understanding of what you are presenting. It is upsetting for a severely handicapped person whose mental ability is normal to be addressed as someone with little understanding. They will appreciate it if music sessions match their intellectual ability and give them something to stimulate their imagination, rather than treat them as babies.

When you enjoy music with mentally handicapped pupils it should be your aim to stretch their ability. Sometimes I have found that pupils are not progressing because I have under-estimated their ability and I expect too little from them. Carol, for instance, enjoyed music sessions when she first began to attend. She attempted to play notes on a xylophone and enjoyed the songs. She could beat the drum but gave up after a very short while. Then she ceased to play an active role in her music group and I wondered why this was so. At the time I was experiencing difficulties with another young woman who demanded 'pop' records continually during sessions and when refused cried and screamed in an endeavour to obtain her own way (it became necessary to hide the record player and records when she came to the room). Having partially sorted out this problem, I introduced Carol to beating the drum twice at the end of each line of the song 'If you're happy and you know it . . .' I did not expect her to be able to do this, but she immediately took an interest and could do it well. Although her speech is extremely limited (mainly 'mummy' and 'baby') she began to attempt to say, 'Here I am' and, 'How are you?' during a song when given time to think about it. As a result of these signs of her ability I introduced her to Makaton sign vocabulary (see page 126) and she surprised everyone by the rapid way she learned signs. One Thursday I showed her five new signs which she copied once. The following Tuesday she signed three of these correctly without prompt or reminder, having had no reminder of them in the intervening days. Sometimes it is necessary to try something more difficult with a pupil or group when they are apparently unable to do something quite simple. They need a challenge in order to encourage them to play an active role and begin to enjoy participation.

If you are working with mentally handicapped young people or adults, be careful not to present them with songs which are babyish in content. Let them see that you respect them, treat them as equals and show that you are willing to work with them enjoying and producing music that is adult in content. Introduce them to a wider and adult way of life through music and help them to understand how to have fun in an adult way.

Additional activities
The following activities may be useful for your pupils, individually or in groups, if they want to learn to play instruments.

Learning to play using colour
If your pupils can recognise colours or are learning to match colours, you could use this ability to aid them in learning to read and play music. You will need to use distinct colours, not including different shades of the same colour. If you can purchase a suitably coloured xylophone this can be used, otherwise use a plain one and put coloured stickers on the appropriate notes. Choose your own order of colour for each note, for example:

(Middle) C – black
         D – red
         E – blue
         F – yellow
         G – brown
         A – green
         B – orange

To distinguish octave C from middle C you could make it a different colour, perhaps white. Write out tunes (in the key of C – no flats or sharps) using these eight notes only, and place coloured stickers according to your colour code above or below each note. For example:

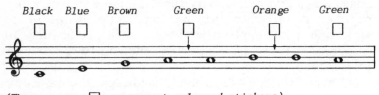

(The squares □ represent coloured stickers)

If you prefer to work from a colour coded teaching set already worked out for you, there are some available from music shops or through catalogues (see Useful Addresses, page 189). Some are more complex, using colour to teach the values of notes.

Learning to play by letter name
Most xylophones have the letter name on each note. If your pupils can recognise or match letters then you can help them to play melodies by writing the letter name under each note of music.

Derek is severely mentally handicapped and epileptic. We were very surprised to find that he could recognise the letter 'D' written on the black board, turn to the xylophone and find it there. Perhaps the letter 'D', being the first letter of his name, had more significance for him. It does show that even a severely mentally handicapped person may be able to learn to play music in this way. Being able to read music can bring to pupils an all too rare sense of achievement.

Group playing by use of chart and symbols
Make a chart with tunes on it (large so that pupils can see it easily) and choose symbols for each note of the scale. Write these symbols above or below the appropriate notes. Make up a set of cards with one symbol per card. For example:

Give a card to each pupil – or two cards if you have a small group of pupils. Provide each pupil with the corresponding chime bar or identify the note to be used on a xylophone (by means of a sticker, by removing the notes either side of the required note, or else by showing the pupil the note and asking him to remember that he is playing 'F' for the 'fish' on his card, or 'B' for the 'bat'). Point to the first symbol and note on the chart. The pupil with the corresponding symbol plays the note. Point to the next symbol and note and the pupil with that symbol plays the next note, and so on.

Painting to music
An interesting way of combining the use of colour and music is to provide your pupils with different coloured paints, brushes and paper and to play music for them while they paint; or to play them a piece of music first and ask them to paint a picture to describe what they have heard. It can be a fascinating experiment to see what effect different types of music have on your pupils and the paintings they produce.

Exploring sounds together
You can enjoy an interesting and happy time with your pupils exploring the sounds made by different things. Encourage them to listen carefully to the sounds made by the different instruments which you have. Explore with them the range of sounds possible. Beat on a large drum, a small drum, a snare drum. Let them experiment with a range of chime bars, playing

the note and holding the bar near their ear. Play excerpts from records to illustrate the sound that is made by instruments such as a pipe organ, flute, violin or bagpipes, or the unusual sounds made on a synthesizer.

Turn their attention to everyday objects and help your pupils to find out what sound each makes. For example: a handful of small coins, one coin dropped on a hard surface, water dripping into a bucket, a kettle boiling or a whistling kettle, wind blowing through trees, the sound made by walking on dry leaves – and so on. Ask your pupils to think of these things which make sounds and try to imitate them vocally. This is an aspect which could keep your pupils interested and occupied for a number of sessions and produce a great deal of discussion (further suggestions can be found in Chapter Nine, Drama and Music).

Improvisation

Using instruments and sounds which you have explored together, make up a piece of music. Together you could choose a theme such as 'Going for a walk', 'A happy day', or 'Dancing'. Using the chosen theme let your pupils decide which instruments they want to play or which of them should make sounds appropriate to the theme. Conduct the group, bringing in the various instruments and increasing or decreasing the volume. If this is working well with a group, they may enjoy making up a longer story expressed only in sound. For example: 'I wake up as the alarm clock rings but fall back to sleep. I wake up again and find that I am late for work. I jump out of bed, rush to the bathroom and have a quick wash, hurry downstairs, boil the kettle and have a cup of tea, slam the door and run all the way to work.' This calls for a great deal of concentration and planning but will be an exhilarating experience for everyone if it is approached in the right manner with pupils who can cope with this type of activity (for further ideas see Chapter Nine, Drama and Music).

Performance

To be able to perform to an audience the music that you have been practising is an exciting experience. Handicapped pupils can experience this too by putting on a concert occasionally for

Left: Solo singing raises confidence and gives a platform for performance.

Right: Despite severe handicaps, listening to music can bring joy.

Below left: Some people act like the proverbial ostrich!

Below right: But involvement in music can make life more interesting.

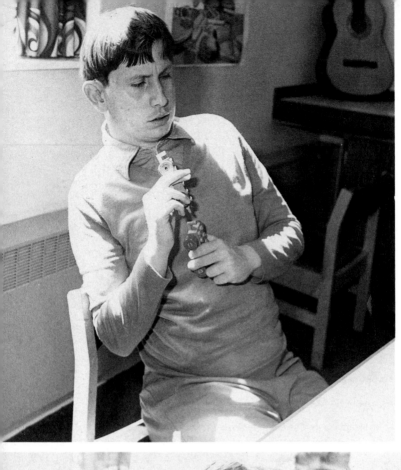

This young ~
used to retre~
from
involvement ~
with other
people . . .

But he
responds to
music and is~
learning to
form
relationships~
a result.

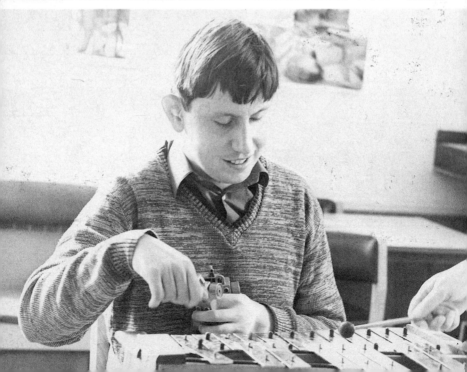

"Shake, shake, shake the bells!"

Beating the drum is an enjoyable occupation which aids development.

It is great fun to make music with a friend's help.

The joy of playing melodies is obvious for this young blind man.

Some handicapped people develop real musical skills.

"Hello, hello, how are you?" Developing awareness and eye contact.

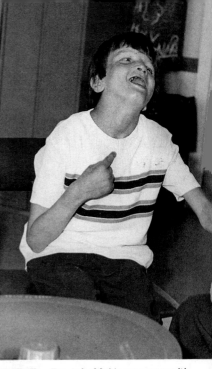

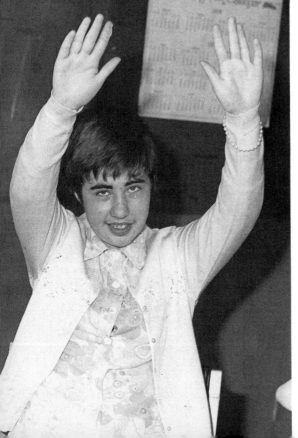

Top left: Making contact with others in the group through a greeting song.

Top right: "Here I am . . ."

Left: Body awareness songs: ". . . shoulders, ARMS and then my head . . ."

"This is my nose . . ."

"With my hands I clap, clap, clap . . ."

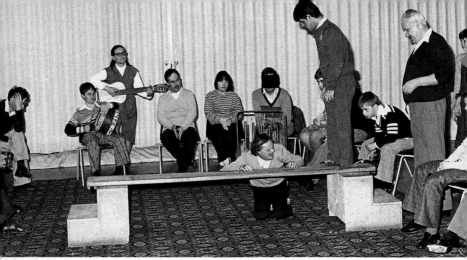

Music and drama: here comes the littlest billy goat.

The middle-sized billy goat meets the troll.

Watch out — here comes the BIG billy goat!

Enjoying a happy time, playing and singing . . .

. . . and generally becoming involved.

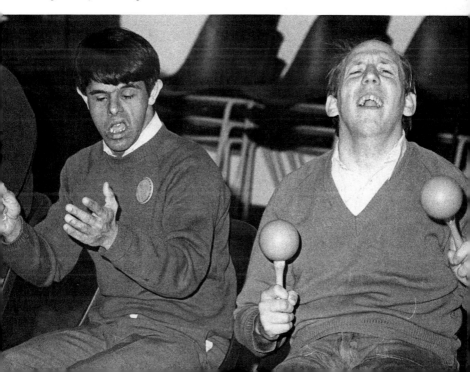

Group involvement in a simple activity.

Although confined to a wheelchair this young woman enjoys action songs.

Movement and music: small circles –

– and large circles.

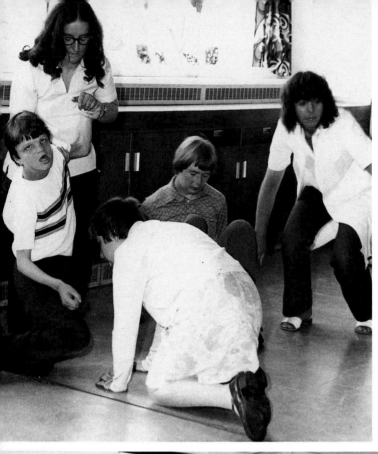

Musical bumps.

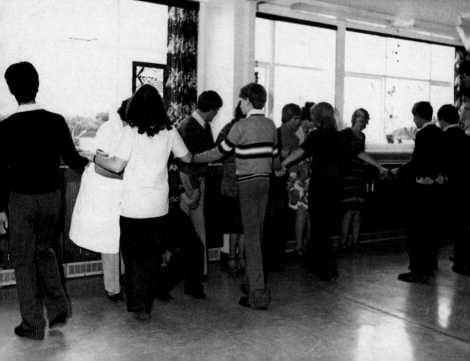

Lines meeting and retreating.

Playing 'trains'.

Increasing awareness and communication . . .   . . . and agility.

Getting down to the job.

Learning to help someone else.

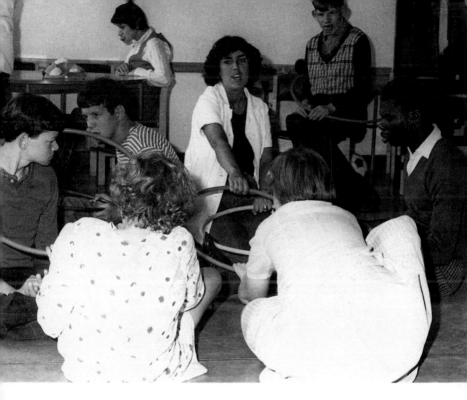

Involvement through the use of hoops.

A song and dance

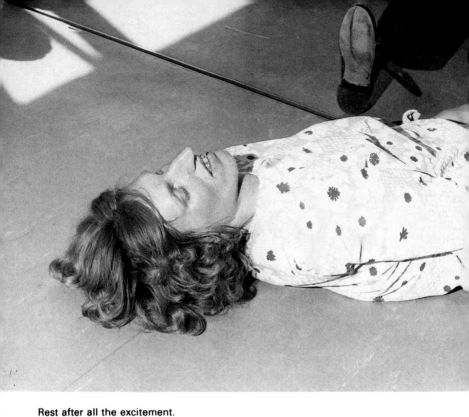

Rest after all the excitement.

Zzzzzzzzz.

parents and friends. Some very severely handicapped pupils may not be able to perform in public as their enjoyment of music may be greater than their ability to participate actively. If such pupils are able to sing or play something, however brief, give them a solo spot, as this will be a great encouragement both to them and to their relatives. All too often handicapped people are on the receiving end and rely on other people to entertain them. For them to be able to give pleasure to other people makes a happy change.

6. LISTENING TO MUSIC

Recorded music versus live music

Listening to recorded music is as far as most people ever go in their involvement with music. They do not sing or play an instrument but they receive a tremendous amount of pleasure from listening to music. It is easier to listen to recorded music at home than to go to a concert hall, and many music lovers do not attend live performances regularly. Yet however excellent the reproduction of music, something is lacking when one listens to tapes or records. Live music creates a vital link between performers and audience, however large the concert hall or how small the room where the performance takes place, and an atmosphere is created which cannot be reproduced.

Music played live by you or someone else on an instrument is far more interesting for your pupils than listening to records. Find out who is available in your locality and invite them to sing or play to your pupils. Young people learning instruments may enjoy visiting your class. The Council for Music in Hospitals arranges for musicians to give concerts suitable for residents in hospitals of various kinds (see Useful Addresses).

There is, however, a case for using recorded music. It is not always easy for handicapped pupils to visit a concert hall because of the lack of suitable transport at the right time, the expense involved, a lack of escorts, too long a performance to sit through, difficulty of access, and so on. So in order to enjoy orchestral or instrumental music which no one local is able to play for your pupils, the next best will be for them to listen to a recording. In addition, by using recorded music they can be introduced to a wide range in a relatively short time, as you will not have to wait for the performance of particular concerts.

Variety of music

When you think of music, what first comes to mind? Some

people never seem to explore further than 'pop' music, and it is only when a piece of classical music strays into the 'pop' charts, or a long playing record of excerpts from classical music becomes very popular, that they notice its existence. If you travel through life never listening to music other than the one kind that you enjoy, you will miss a great deal and will have less to share with your pupils. You may be surprised to find that you enjoy types of music that you have not listened to before. Have you listened to and shared with your pupils any of the following? Folk songs (English, Welsh, Scottish, Irish – each has its own particular flavour, before you even consider the folk songs of other countries). Folk dance music – this likewise presents tremendous scope. Ballet music. Operatic music. Oratorio – musical settings of religious themes. Mediæval music played on authentic instruments. Chants – such as were used through the centuries by monastic orders. Vocal solos sung by sopranos, contraltos, tenors, bass and other voices. Orchestral music. Instrumental and vocal duets, trios, quartets, quintets, etc. Atonal music. Pipe or theatre organ music. These are just a few of the different kinds and combinations of music available for you and your pupils to share and enjoy.

Reaction to music

When I first began playing music to groups of pupils, it surprised me that even very severely mentally handicapped people showed definite likes and dislikes. The majority rarely heard anything other than nursery rhymes or 'pop' music from day to day, yet they still showed preference or dislike for other types of music.

For example, Terry came to music regularly over a period of a year or so. He is a very severely mentally handicapped young man, physically able bodied, but preferring to sit all day and objecting to being moved or fed. He registers his disapproval by biting his hand or slapping his head and wailing. In music he was unwilling to participate in any way and showed no interest in activities. We began to introduce the group to various types of music and to note their reaction. 'Pop' music upset Terry and he began biting his hand and wailing loudly. The rest of the group enjoyed a 'country and western' song, but not Terry. But when we played classical organ and orchestral music to him, his reaction was remarkable. He stood up and wandered dreamily around the room, gazing up at the ceiling, smiling to himself, completely taken up by the beauty of the music. Each time we played this type of music he reacted in the same way, apart from one occasion when he was already very upset by something that had happened before the lesson, and the music failed to penetrate his mood.

Josie disliked anything but 'pop' music and caused a great commotion if she could not have it on. By introducing other types of music into the sessions she gradually learned to tolerate certain pieces. One of these was 'Mars' from the *Planets Suite* – which matched her defiance!

Sion is a Downs Syndrome young man of very low ability who relies on others for all his needs and has no speech. He shows pleasure by laughing and when he cries he looks so miserable that it is almost impossible not to cry with him! He tends to explore cupboards and tip up things, much as a small child does. Nevertheless, he enjoys 'pop' tunes and lively military music and taps his foot to it, and he also loves orchestral and choir music and will sit very still for long periods listening to it with his eyes focused on the record deck.

A calming influence

On days when pupils are noisy or upset (things often seem worse on rainy days!) I use a quiet piece of piano music or soothing recorded music to calm the situation. Choose music carefully and keep it ready for such occasions, assessing its effectiveness with your particular pupils.

A record club

A good way of introducing your pupils to a variety of music is to form a record club. You could begin by asking them to bring a favourite record for the group to listen to and encouraging them to say why they enjoy it (but do not exclude pupils who have little or no speech). Introduce other records into sessions and build up a list from which they can choose to listen again. This is particularly suitable for adults who are mildly mentally handicapped and for physically handicapped people.

Something to avoid

Ice cream is delicious – some children think that they would like to live on it. Chocolates are lovely – but even I begin to lose interest in them after indulging in a boxful. Music is delightful – but played all day, every day, it can become tiresome.

Plan music sessions for your pupils which last a specific time, and then have other activities for them to do. Some of your pupils may live in a situation where loudspeakers play music to them all day and they have no choice but to listen. Others may be physically unable to turn sound on and off without aid. It is cruel to subject people to continuous music without finding out if they want it and what they like, particularly if they are not allowed to leave the environment or are unable to move. Music may be provided for them out of kindness, but lack of thought in presentation can produce the opposite effect. If you have any influence on this situation, suggest quiet times in between and a variety in the music played. Suggest interspersing music with stories suitable for the age and experience of those listening.

Research into music for listening has been conducted by music therapist Anthony Wigram and is available from the British Society for Music Therapy (see Useful Addresses).

7: LET'S WRITE SONGS

It is often difficult to find exactly the right songs for use with handicapped pupils, although some songs may well be suitable if your pupils are physically handicapped but of average intelligence for their age. Many children's songs are attractive to mentally handicapped pupils, but however simple the theme of the songs, very often too many words are used and ideas expressed which they cannot be expected to understand. Moreover, as these pupils grow towards adulthood they need songs with meaningful words which express their feelings and outlook on life. The best solution is for you to write such songs with your own pupils in mind, so that the word content and the views expressed are easily understood by them. It may also be possible for your pupils to learn to make up their own songs with your aid. I shall consider this later in the chapter.

How to write songs

You may think that song writing is something that you could never do, but if you have not tried to write a song before it may surprise you to find how easy it really is. If you experience difficulties for any reason, keep trying, and one day you may suddenly find that it has become very simple.

Let me explain the way to write a song that I find easiest. You may find this method suitable or discover a way which suits you better. Think of something that you want to teach or share with your pupils, for example, 'time'. Think around the word and consider what it suggests to you. Time: to get up – to go out – to eat dinner – to have a bath – and so on. Choose the most suitable ideas and start writing, linking these ideas together. If you are able to write poetry you have a head start. If not, you can still write songs whose words may not necessarily rhyme beautifully but can be put to music and express what is required. For instance, you could write one verse of the 'time' song like this:

> At six o'clock in the morning
> I wake up, I wake up.
> At six o'clock in the morning
> I wake up and get out of my bed.

Read it aloud and get a feeling for the rhythm of the words. You may find that a tune is beginning to develop in your mind as you read it. Sit down at the piano (or use any pitched instrument) and make up a tune to suit the words, using the eight white notes up from middle C. Write down the letter names of the notes you use as you go along. Play it right through and sing the words. If you need to do so, change a note here and there until you are reasonably satisfied. For example:

> At six o'clock in the morning
> C   C   C   C   C   A   G   E
> I wake up, I wake up.
> C   D   G   D   E   G
> At six o'clock in the morning
> C   C   C   C   C   A   G   E
> I wake up and get out of my bed.
> C   D   E   D   E   F   E   D   C

This is all you need to write down if you cannot write musical notation and are not familiar with the value of notes. Practise it until you are certain of it and you have the rhythm fixed in your mind. If you think you may forget it, make a tape recording of yourself singing it for future reference. You can then use it with your pupils. Play the melody line and sing it to your pupils or (as described in Chapter One) play the melody with your left hand as well but eight notes lower than your right hand. If you want it written out in musical notation and you are not sure how to do it, ask someone who can write it out for you. Perhaps they will also be able to add harmony for you. You will be thrilled to find that you have the ability to write your own songs as you need them, and it will save you many hours of searching for suitable songs for your pupils.

Examples of songs

In this chapter I am including a number of songs that I have written for mentally handicapped pupils. One difficulty that some of the pupils have is knowing which day of the week it is, so I wrote a song using the names of the days to help them remember. When using it with them we link the days to various activities. For example:

Sunday: William's mother takes him out in the car.
Monday: we use the 'free expression room' (sand and water play).
Tuesday: Drama Club is held in the evening.
Wednesday: Ron misses music to go to the Recreation Hall.
Thursday: is 'Top of the Pops' (on T.V. in the evening).
Friday: we have more music (double session).
Saturday: some pupils go shopping.

You will be able to link particular activities in your own pupils' week to the names of the days.

Another song is about the weather. Some pupils rarely consider what the weather is like, so we sing a song about the weather, encourage them to look out of the window, feel if it is raining or look up for the sun in the sky. Make sketches of the different kinds of weather conditions to aid identification, for discussion or to be used by pupils who have no speech. Songs about different kinds of weather are fun (see 'Snow' and 'Wind' on pages 116–18). Your pupils will love to hear them or sing them themselves, especially if you make them live by really enjoying them yourself.

The 'Teeth Cleaning Song' in Chapter Four was written by members of an 'A' level music class at a local school. Some of the pupils from the school visit our pupils weekly as part of a work experience programme. You may find that a local school's music department will be interested in a song writing project. It will give them an insight into the needs of other people and practice in writing music.

You may find it useful to write a song such as 'Beat the Drum'.

Your pupils will enjoy songs about food. After singing this song you can discuss with them the food they like best, what food they eat for breakfast, dinner or tea, what they would take

BEAT THE DRUM

Key of: C Major

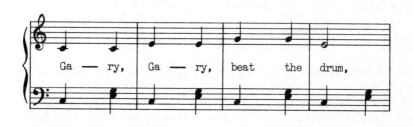

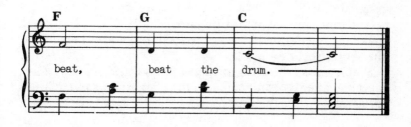

on a picnic, and so on. This will help them to name food correctly and to make choices. For pupils who have no speech make drawings of food so that they can participate in the discussion.

The song 'A Ride in the Car' also includes choice. You could make up any number of verses to include going to the seaside, the shops, for a walk, etc.

Songs about the days of the week and the weather can be used day after day and continue to be interesting and a means of learning.

I LIKE FOOD

Key of: C Major

I   like   to   eat. ————

A RIDE IN THE CAR

Where shall we go for a

ride in our car? Where

shall we go?

Shall we go to the Zoo to-

WHAT DAY IS IT?

When singing about weather conditions it is interesting to have songs about specific weather, such as snow, wind or rain.

THE WEATHER SONG

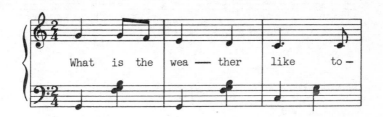

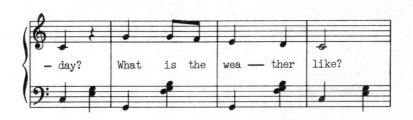

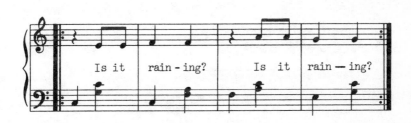

It is a rain—y day to—day!

SNOW

Key of: C Major

It's win — ter, and it's snow - ing!

Brr ————————————— Ev - ery-thing is

white, I think I'll build a

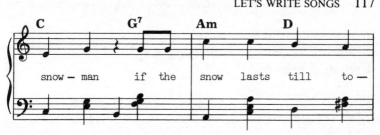

snow — man   if the   snow   lasts   till   to —

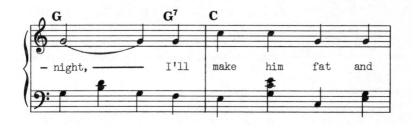

— night, ———— I'll   make   him   fat   and

build   him   tall, I'll   give   him   a   stick   and   a

scarf   as   well.   It's   snow — ing! ————

WINDY DAY

Key of: D Major

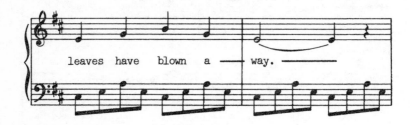

Additional verses:

   Button up my coat, to keep the cold wind out
   Ooooh . . .

and with a little adjustment to fit the music:

   Shut the windows, shut the doors, keep the wind out
   when it roars.
   Ooooh . . .

COLOUR SONG

Key of: C Major

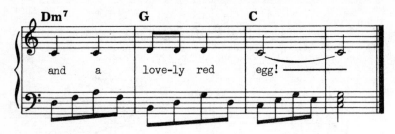

The colour song is useful if you have plenty of colour around the room. The egg referred to in it was an egg-shaped piece of tinfoil fixed to the wall.

Songs about events always catch the imagination and help in anticipating what will happen. See the Christmas song opposite. Additional verses:

> Father Christmas will come here, will come here.
> Father Christmas will come here,
> But it's not Christmas today.
>
> He will bring some presents . . .
>
> We will all have Christmas cake . . .
>
> We will eat some mince pies . . .

and so on.

Another example is the song for Fireworks Night, given on page 122. Additional verses can be added:

> The fireworks go bang, bang, whoosh . . .
> And fly up to the sky.
>
> The bonfire will burn so bright . . .
> And keep us nice and warm.

Songs for the end of sessions can be written to suit the particular occasion – whether one is meeting every day or weekly, etc.

CHRISTMAS

Key of: C Major

FIREWORKS NIGHT

Key of: C Major

Soon it will be fire — works night!

Fire — works night! Fire — works night!

Soon it will be fire — works night and

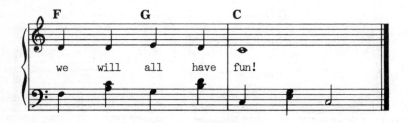

we will all have fun!

GOODBYE SONG

Key of: C Major

Writing songs with your pupils

When you have gained a little confidence in writing songs yourself, perhaps you would like to encourage your pupils to write their own songs. They will be able to make a greater or lesser contribution according to their ability. One pupil may suggest a title for a song and have little further to add. Another may say a few words that can be included. Write down all the suggestions and then ask for ideas for the melody. Perhaps they will want to work it out for themselves on an instrument, or they may hum or sing a phrase or the outline of the whole song. Write it down making as few alterations as possible. Throughout the process, make the song theirs, not yours. If one pupil writes a song, always refer to it as his song. Do not take credit for songs yourself if you write them with your pupils in this way.

Roy walked into the music room one day when a group had failed to arrive. He is an obstinate young man who is mentally handicapped. He has epilepsy with frequent 'absences' which make it difficult to know whether he is having a fit or if he is refusing to answer questions or obey commands. His conversation is repetitious and he finds it difficult to reply to questions. He does not mix very well and needs one-to-one attention for activities if he is to derive any enjoyment from them. On the day in question he became interested in beating the drum. As he did so, he sang a few words about Christmas. I encouraged him to continue and asked him if he would like to write a song. This appealed to him so I wrote the words he suggested and we sang the melody together. He became very happily involved in this and wholeheartedly accepted the song as his. He wanted a copy of the words to take away with him, so I wrote it down, entitling it 'Roy's Song'. These are the words of his final version:

> I like Father Christmas,
> Do you like him too?
> He's a fat man,
> He's a nice man,
> He has toys for you.
> I like Father Christmas,
> Do you like him too?

Everyone has a need to experience success in their lives. By writing and performing their own songs, handicapped people can feel a sense of achievement which can add so much to their enjoyment of life.

The Makaton Vocabulary

Some of my pupils are learning to sign as they are unable to speak or have very limited or indistinct speech. When we found that they enjoyed signing, we began to sign words they had learnt which appeared in songs. To make it more enjoyable and worthwhile for them, we wrote songs using as few other words as possible in order to emphasise the words that we wanted them to sign. When these songs were sung, even the pupils who were normally reluctant to sign joined in, unprompted, with their fellow signers.

The Makaton Vocabulary began in 1972 in Surrey, as a project to teach sign language to deaf mentally handicapped adults. It was soon revised for use with children and has become the system used to stimulate language development in the majority of ESN(S) schools in Great Britain. Makaton is the applied use of a specific development vocabulary; it has been designed to provide a controlled method of teaching signs from the British Sign Language to mentally handicapped children and adults and other language handicapped people, in order to provide a basic means of communication; to encourage expressive speech wherever possible; to develop an understanding of language through the visual medium of the signs and logical structure of the sign language. (From a statement by Walker and Armfield, Makaton Development Project, 1981, *Special Education: Forward Trends*, Vol. 8, No. 3.)

I have had the privilege of working with a speech therapist in teaching Makaton to groups of mentally handicapped adults. Despite the severity of their handicap, they have been able to learn a number of signs which allow them to express themselves in a way that had previously been impossible for them. For example, they can sign 'drink' if they are thirsty, or ask for a biscuit. They can use the sign for 'bed' to say that they are tired, or they can ask to go to the toilet. As music is motivating for these pupils it seemed logical to combine music and Makaton by writing special Makaton songs.

We have noticed a marked improvement in the behaviour and awareness of pupils who have begun to learn to sign. It is very interesting to see them on occasions sitting by themselves, signing to themselves much as a little child tries out the words he has learnt to say. For pupils with more ability the use of

Makaton opens up a new world. When I first knew Norris it concerned me that he had so much he wished to say but was unable to express in words. He would take staff aside and try so hard to tell them something, or he would point out of the window and the task would begin of naming everything in sight until he nodded in agreement. The use of Makaton has even helped some pupils to speak, as concentration on a limited number of words helps them to say them as well as sign.

Makaton songs
Here are some songs I wrote using words from the first stage of Makaton. The Makaton Vocabulary Development Project also has songs available (see Useful Addresses). If you are using Makaton with your pupils, why not try using songs to reinforce the learning of signs? If the parents of pupils also learn the songs, they can be sung at home. Care staff in hostels or care units will be encouraged to use the signs if they learn the songs to sing with those in their care.

GOOD MORNING

Key of: C Major

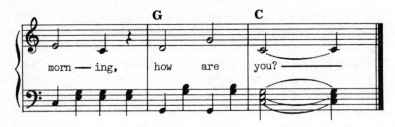

DRINK – BISCUIT

Key of: F Major

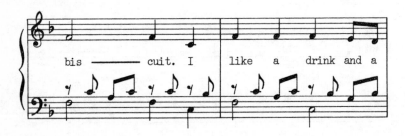

TOILET

Key of: F Major

Where   is   the   toi —— let?

Where   is   the   toi —— let? ——

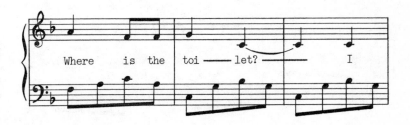

Where   is   the   toi —— let? ——   I

need a toi — let now!

THE BUS

Key of: C Major

Here comes the bus to take us for a ride! The bus, the bus, to take us for a ride! Hur —

- rah!   Hur - rah!   The bus,   the

bus,   here   comes the bus   to

take   us   for   a   ride!

GO TO BED

Key of: C Major

rest   your   head,   rest your   head,

rall.

go   to   bed.

8:   MUSIC TO MOVE

Music lives through movement, for it is by moving from note to note and phrase to phrase that it is created. Certain styles of music give us more feeling of movement than others. When listening to them we feel compelled to get up and move, march or dance.

Many handicapped people lack movement. They may be unmotivated, or find movement difficult because of physical problems and prefer to sit all day. There is also the other extreme – hyperactive mentally handicapped persons, or physically handicapped people who are determined not to be outdone by able bodied friends. The use of movement to music can be beneficial in all circumstances, encouraging movement for the less motivated and providing a framework for movement which produces order out of chaos for hyperactive pupils, or provides an outlet for a superabundance of energy.

Exploring patterns for group movement
You will find that arranging movement exercises to music for groups of pupils is a fascinating and most enjoyable experience. There is a wide field waiting to be explored by you and your pupils and plenty of scope to develop your own programmes. What you develop to suit your pupils will be unique. Here are some ideas for exercises to music to help you as you think about planning your programmes.

Marching
This is a basic exercise that you can use with groups of pupils. There is an abundance of music in march time from which to choose. If you do not have anyone able to provide live music for your movement sessions, use recorded music. You may wish to use a different piece of music each session, or change it once a week or month. You may decide to keep the same piece

for a long period so that the particular piece of music means 'let's march'.

You can use your imagination, and so can your pupils, to decide what form the marching will take. You may choose to march around the room, clockwise or anticlockwise, to march across the room, turn and march back again, or to march between obstacles. You may prefer 'musical bumps' – sitting down when the music stops and marching again when it restarts. You can encourage the more able pupils to aid the less able or reluctant ones to join in. If all your pupils have little ability you will need at least one helper to two pupils in order to encourage participation. Pupils in wheelchairs need not be excluded from the enjoyment of the activity. They can be pushed around the room and feel involved in the session. Alternatively the wheelchairs and occupants could be placed around the room and the ambulant pupils march around or between the chairs, greeting the occupants as they pass. This is a light hearted exercise which everyone can join in and enjoy to the full.

Marching

Circles

Hold hands with your pupils to form a circle. Explore what you can do with a circle. You may move to the right, move to the left, walk to the centre and out again, you can swing your arms and legs. You can break the circle at one point and wind into the centre and out again.

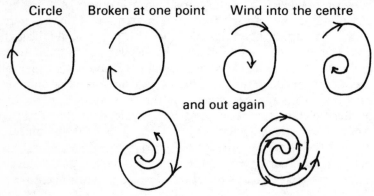

You may like to make a large circle with wheelchairs in the centre so that the physically handicapped pupils can see what everyone else is doing and form the focal point of the circle.

By breaking the circle at one point the leader can trace various shapes with the rest of the group following. End by resuming the circle.

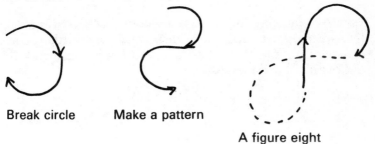

Break circle   Make a pattern

A figure eight

Alternatively the circle can stand still while one or two pupils walk in and out of the circle under the arms of those forming it. Perhaps you will be able to think of other activities using circles that your pupils will enjoy.

In and out of a stationary circle

Lines
Instead of making a circle, form two lines of pupils facing each other across the room. Choose music that has a definite pattern

and a suitable pace which tells the pupils when to move forwards and backwards. Here are some suggestions for activities with lines.

Pupils comprising line 1 advance upon line 2 and opposite individuals greet each other, then walk backwards to their original positions. Line 2 advances to line 1 and then walks backwards to base, and so on.

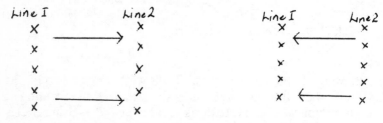

or

Both lines walk forward to meet in the centre, greet each other and walk backwards to base. Repeat this movement thoughout the exercise which should last for one or two minutes.

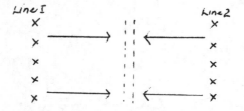

or

Lines 1 and 2 walk forward to meet at the centre. Line 1 pupils raise their arms to form arches and line 2 pupils pass under and continue across the room. Repeat the exercise with lines passing under or forming arches alternately.

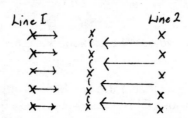

or

Form four lines in a square (or have at least two persons on each of four sides).

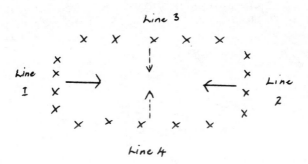

Lines 1 and 2 walk to the centre, greet each other and retreat backwards to base. Lines 3 and 4 walk to the centre and likewise return to base. Continue these movements until the end of the exercise. The music chosen to accompany these exercises should be of a suitable length and with the right rhythm to make the exercises flow easily.

Under and over

Your pupils will enjoy an 'obstacle race' to music. Plan the layout of the course to suit your pupils and the space available. You could choose to form a 'train', with the pupils holding each other at the waist. Make an arch or tunnel out of foam shapes for the 'train' to pass under or use pairs of pupils or helpers joining hands. Perform the exercise to a song about a train or to music which resembles the movement of a train.

Alternatively, lay out the course to include a low form to walk along on one side of the room, a table to crawl under on the other side, steps up and down on a third side and foam shapes to step over on the fourth side. Provide an opportunity for more able pupils to aid the others around the course. Lively music for this exercise will keep the activity moving and make it a happy time.

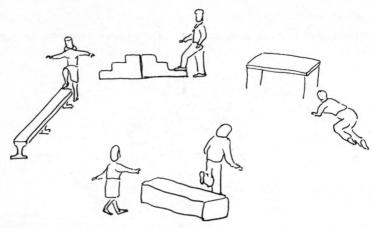

Rocking

Ask your pupils to sit on the floor in pairs, or one pupil with a helper, facing each other. With hands linked, rock backwards and forwards in time to music which has an easy rocking rhythm.

Ready to rock   Backwards and forwards

If your pupils are too timid to sit facing another person so closely, use a hoop between each pair, as this will contrive a less threatening encounter.

Holding a hoop   Stretching backwards and forwards

For pupils in wheelchairs, position them in pairs holding a hoop between them and encourage them to pull and push each other gently forwards and backwards. If your pupils are not able to do this, arrange for a helper (staff or another pupil) to hold a hoop with the pupils. With the brakes released push the wheelchair gently backwards and then draw it forwards using the hoop.

It can also be fun to sit back to back with a pupil and rock from side to side, with hands used to push on the floor at either side. You can also lean backwards or forwards with your partner. If you sit back to back and make sounds, (cough, grunt or speak) these can be felt as well as heard by your partner.

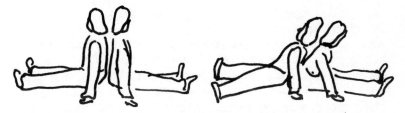

Passing objects around
Sit with your pupils in a circle on the floor or on chairs. As the music is played pass objects from person to person around the circle. Pass either a large object and a small one, a soft object and a hard one, or two objects which make different sounds, and so on, for contrast and to increase awareness. Pass these objects in the same direction or in opposite directions according to ability. Give verbal commands such as, 'Give this to David,' or, 'Give me the box,' to aid participation and to increase understanding of verbal commands.

Relaxation
Some music gives more of a feeling of relaxation than others.

When it is played you feel like sinking into an easy chair and allowing the cares of the world to pass you by, or you imagine yourself lying in the sun on a beautiful beach with not a care in the world. Choose this type of music for your pupils and encourage them to lie down quietly with you and listen to it. Provide mats or blankets to lie on, or lie on the floor if it is carpeted and comfortably warm. If a pupil is unwilling to lie down or be quiet, sit with him, smooth his hair, whisper or sing softly to him or stroke his hands and arms. It is important that any helpers present should join in by lying down quietly themselves and not engage in conversation with others while the music is played.

Noisy and boisterous pupils will need time and perseverance from you in order to learn that it is enjoyable to lie down and relax for a few minutes. Some groups with whom I have worked have appeared totally unable to relax, yet over a period of months have learnt to remain quiet for the duration of the music. Those assisting often say that these are the best few minutes of the day! After all, it is not often one is paid to lie down and do nothing!

Including pupils in wheelchairs
Each of the above activities can involve pupils in wheelchairs to a greater or lesser degree. During the 'marching' exercise wheelchairs can be pushed around the room or the able bodied pupils can march around the wheelchairs, thus making the physically handicapped pupils an essential part of the activity. If those in wheelchairs are able to walk at all with aid, this is a good opportunity for them to be out of their chairs and walking around the room. If they use walking aids encourage them to participate. During the circle exercise pupils in wheelchairs can be placed in the centre so that they can watch others taking part. Again, if able to walk a little they can be supported by helpers on either side of them in the circle. Pupils in wheelchairs can be included in the 'lines' exercise too. Wheelchairs can be pushed forwards and backwards as part of a line with ambulant pupils, or if you have a large group in wheelchairs make up a line entirely of wheelchairs. The 'under and over' activity is a little more difficult. Wheelchairs will go under an arch but not over an object so they must miss out part

of the exercise. When 'rocking', hoops may be used as described earlier to involve those unable to sit on the floor or to balance well enough to hold a hoop or another person's hands. During the 'relaxation' exercise, if your pupils are easy to lift out of their wheelchairs, place them on the floor during this activity and help them to relax their limbs and stretch out as a change from the sitting position to which they are accustomed.

Frequency and duration of sessions
It is ideal if you can plan to have a short session of exercises each day. If this is not possible, try to have a session at least once a week. The time taken for sessions will vary according to your pupils' ability. You may find that you will need to introduce one exercise at a time, beginning with a few minutes' marching around the room, and in stages introduce other exercises as your pupils learn to enjoy group movement. A set of exercises lasting fifteen to twenty minutes can be quite sufficient. It is far better to have a short and happy session than one that drags on and becomes very tiring. Sessions should be looked forward to with eager anticipation, not thought of as something to be endured.

Individual movement for pupils with physical disabilities
As described in Chapter Four, Enjoyment One-to-One, exercises can be designed for pupils who are physically handicapped. These exercises can be used in a group setting provided that there are sufficient helpers available for one person to work with one pupil. When there is a group it is more enjoyable for the pupils as they can see other pupils moving too. Do make sure that you consult each pupil's doctor or physiotherapist before beginning these exercises, to make certain that they are suitable for a particular individual.

A song book with exercises, the *Goldie Leigh Song Book*, which you may find suitable when working with groups of physically handicapped pupils, is available from the Nordoff-Robbins Music Therapy Centre (see Useful Addresses).

Folk dancing
From moving around a room to music it is but a short step to

dancing to the music. Folk dancing can provide many happy hours for pupils and bring involvement with other people who are interested in folk dancing. Because folk dancing is a mode of expression which has been passed down through generations and has evolved according to the pattern of life, it is very adaptable to all situations.

In ancient times the unbroken circle was considered the perfect shape, and there are many circle dances to be found which are interesting and varied. A broken circle with a leader can direct the group into 'a merry dance'. Dances involving lines and squares make up all kinds of interesting sequences. Folk dancing involves music as an accompaniment. Your pupils may either enjoy dancing or making an accompaniment for their fellow pupils to dance to. This can consist of hand clapping, tapping the feet or singing, as well as the use of instruments. Because it is 'folk', there need be no set rules and you can design your own dances to suit the ability of your pupils.

Security

– Extension

–Merriment

A merry dance

1. *A circle dance*
Hold hands in a circle. To the rhythm of a slow 4/4 beat, walk the circle in one direction for a couple of phrases, stop, turn and then walk in the opposite direction. When pupils are used to this it can be skipped rather than walked. Still holding hands, move into the centre of the circle, which can cause

merriment as everyone meets in the centre. Walk backwards until the circle is extended to its limits. These actions can be repeated again and again in whatever order you decide.

2. *A double circle*

Form two circles, one within the other. As the music begins the outer circle moves to the left while the inner circle moves to the right. Change direction and repeat this as often as you like. Pupils in the inner circle can then take as their partners pupils who are next to them in the outer circle. These partners can 'promenade' round in a circle, turn and 'promenade' back to the starting point. Partners can either hold hands or cross hands in a 'skater's waltz' style. An addition to this dance could be the partners dancing towards and away from each other, or everyone putting one hand into the centre to form a wheel. Your pupils may enjoy a simplified version of the 'Gay Gordons' which is also a double circle.

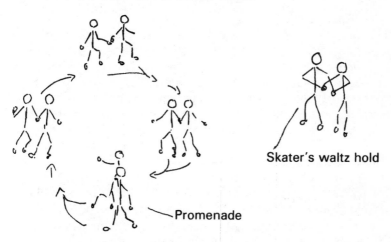

Skater's waltz hold

Promenade

3. *A longways set*

A longways set of four or five couples is a little more complicated. Try a popular Hoe Down Square Dance.

a. Hands held in two lines facing, advance and retire twice (4 steps on each).

b. Drop hands and meet partner, swing around and return to own place twice (8).

c.   Advance to partner, pass back to back and walk back-
     wards to own place twice (8).
     (Figure c. is called 'Dos-a-Dos' – back to back).
d.   The top couple then lead down the centre of the set (4) back
     up (4) and lead their own line down the outside making an
     arch at the bottom under which the others go to reform the
     two lines with a new top couple, the old couple staying at
     the bottom.
     a. to d. can be repeated as often as the dancers wish. Many
     variations are both possible and desirable. (See diagrams
     opposite).

If you can progress this far with folk dancing with your pupils,
why not get in touch with your local Folk Dance Society? They
will most likely be very willing to visit you and put on a display
for you, and will be interested to see your pupils dance and
to dance with them.

Wheelchair dancing
The enjoyment of pupils confined to wheelchairs need not be
limited to watching others dance. Through the work of the
Wheelchair Dance Association they are able to enjoy dancing
to the full in their own right. The Association encourages co-
operation between member clubs and promotes wheelchair
dancing in all its forms. It also collects and publishes
information about wheelchair dancing, offers advice and help
to member clubs and runs courses to instruct wheelchair users
and teachers, as well as raising funds to further the objectives of
the Association. Dance Festivals are held each year with classes
for teams of varying ability and age. The Festivals are held in
the North and the South of England, and in Wales and Scotland.
    Here are two examples of dances. Books of dances and a list
of the terms used are available from the Association.

Friendly Waltz
(Danced to the 'Cuckoo Waltz')

Start in circle facing middle, woman on man's left.
Forward two beats, back two beats.
Woman pass round front of man to finish on the right facing
outwards, four beats.

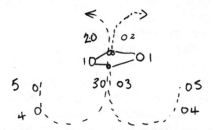

1.   A longways dance for five couples (a)

2.   Leaders (1) lead down outside their own line (d)

3.   Leaders make an arch. No. 2 become the new leaders by
moving up under the arch (d)

4.   Ready to repeat the dance (d–a)

Woman TOS to left, man going around her to finish on her left both facing the middle of circle, eight beats.
Keep repeating until end of music; on each repeat man should have a new partner.

Isle of Skye
(Tune – original)
Longways dance for three couples.

Start facing partner.
A. 'Set' to partner twice (sharp angle right, face, sharp angle left, face.)
    Cross over passing right.
    'Set' twice to partner, cross over passing left.
B. First couple down centre, turn and come up again, turn to face second couple, who have now turned to face up.
C. First and second couples 'set' twice, then woman swing woman, man swing man, $1\frac{1}{2}$ times, to finish facing partner. First couple in second place, second couple are in first place.
    Repeat with third couple moving up dance and swinging with first couple (who will be in second position).

If your pupils are not able to use their own wheelchairs unaided or are unable to understand the instructions, it is very effective if teachers or helpers learn the dances and push the chairs to the music. Your pupils will then be able to experience the fun of dancing together without the need to be able to manoeuvre their own chairs.

Educational Rhythmics
Educational Rhythmics are a series of exercises to music designed to aid physically and mentally handicapped children and young people, and they are also useful for those who have emotional problems. They can be used and enjoyed by children who have no specific problems, and because they are fun to do, learning is accelerated. Although this is movement therapy, the music used with the exercises has a great influence and plays an important part in the programme. The records which accompany the exercises consist of music only. Parents, teachers or

the children themselves can sing or speak the words which are printed in the book. Educational Rhythmics entice the whole child to develop movement, often including speech.

Jennet and Ferris Robins, who developed the system, describe how it grew:

> We have been guided by the desire to help handicapped children and found a valuable solution in the application of co-ordinated movement, with educational themes, in conjunction with music . . . Educational Rhythmics grew out of years of experience in the United States of America and achieved its further development through practical application in many European countries, especially in Switzerland. The simplicity of this method produces an enthusiastic reaction among the young pupils who, in many cases, showed impressive and unexpectedly quick progress in their motoric and intellectual development. (See Reading List, page 187).

Five day workshops run by the authors are held in many different countries including in recent times courses in Ireland, Germany and Belgium (the book is translated into French, German and Norwegian).

The rhythmics described in the manual (*Educational Rhythmics for Mentally and Physically Handicapped Children*) are accompanied by a set of records and include exercises for teaching balance, colours, counting, directions, rhythm, time and so on. A section towards the end of the book deals with additional ideas for using rhythmics with physically handicapped, deaf and blind pupils. Its teaching should be flexible, adapting the exercises to suit individual needs. The authors state:

> Educational Rhythmics is NOT rigid. One should think of this entire method as a basic foundation, which has the possibility of growing and improving with each teacher's individual efforts and abilities.

In Britain these ideas were promoted by the British Institute of Mental Handicap (now the British Institute of Learning Disabilities). Regular workshops were conducted all over Britain for teachers, nurses, care assistants, parents and anyone interested in rhythmics, by a tutor from the Institute. She adapted some exercises, introduced others and had special music written to aid the activities. During a Day Course she would ask her students, who in turn taught their pupils, to work through marching exercises for co-ordination and motor control, clapping exercises which aid awareness of rhythm and numbers, and skills with flags which develop balance, sequence, visual and spatial awareness and which can stimulate basic self-help skills such as dressing, feeding and hair grooming.

Examples of the exercises are as follows:

> These are my ears and I have two,
> These are my eyes and I see you,
> This is my chin that moves to talk,
> And I use my legs to take a walk . . .

> Here's my mouth I talk through.
> I use my ears to hear you.
> Here's my nose to breathe in air.
> My eyes see the world so fair.
> With my hands I touch you.
> On my foot I put my shoe,
> My legs and arms move one by one.
> First I walk and then I run.

> The stork has wings instead of hands
> And sometimes on one leg he stands.
> I wonder if it can be done
> To change one leg to the other one.

The tutor saw these exercises as an important means of stimulating movement and developing co-ordination and synchronisation of purposeful body movements in response to verbal instructions, visual demonstration and music. Using this method she trained pupils who had learning disabilities. Out of her work grew participation for these young people in pantomime, carnivals and open-day displays which incorporated many of the skills developed in Educational Rhythmics sessions. This brought much enjoyment to them and their audiences.

Anyone interested in the use of Educational Rhythmics may obtain the original books and tapes from Switzerland or Ireland (see Useful Addresses) as the British courses are no longer run.

9: DRAMA AND MUSIC

Drama is an enjoyable activity which can bring variety and meaning into the lives of handicapped people. It gives the opportunity for latent abilities to be discovered and is a means of expression for those who may have little chance of expressing themselves meaningfully in other ways. When music is added to drama we have a further dimension and the enjoyment and benefits from participation are increased.

It is often difficult for handicapped people to take part in drama sessions with able bodied groups, and from the point of view of performance it is hard for an audience to disregard the fact that someone is in a wheelchair or is blind, if this is not part of the story line. Some people with a physical handicap, however, do succeed in this respect. For example, one young man, determined to make acting a career, joined an amateur dramatic group. Later he worked with a group of disabled actors who have now become professional. He is now making a career for himself in plays and films alongside able bodied actors.

Drama sessions for your pupils can be held regularly either to prepare a play for performance or as a workshop where interesting activities happen each session and are complete in themselves. The following are some ideas for the use of drama and music during such sessions.

Acting out a story
Your pupils most likely enjoy listening to a story and then acting it, either when it is read a second time or while they retell it in their own words. Provide instruments for them so that they may choose sounds to represent characters and events in the story. Allow them to choose the sounds they think most suitable. This will aid them in listening more carefully to sounds which occur around them, in addition to increasing

their interest in the drama activities. For example, you might read the story of the 'Billy Goats Gruff' to your pupils. Let them choose sounds to represent the river flowing under the bridge, the little billy goat, the middle-sized billy goat, the biggest billy goat and the ugly troll. Choose some pupils to play the instruments which represent the sounds and characters and others to act out the story. The story can be acted several times during a session if you have a large group of pupils, so that more of them will have a chance to take a turn with the instruments or as a character. Those who are very shy may readily play an instrument and thereby be involved in the session, whereas actually standing up and acting a part would be too much for them initially.

Sounds

The range of sounds made by everyday objects, as well as less familiar things, is surprising. Take time with your pupils to listen and explore together. If you are producing a play it can be great fun to provide sound effects as well as music to accompany it. If you are working on different activities each time you meet, sounds can form part of your work, regularly or occasionally as you choose. Ask your pupils, if they are able, to bring objects that make sounds, such as empty containers refilled with rice or dried peas. Let them listen to the rustle of dried grasses. Make ice cubes and listen with your pupils to the sound they make knocking against one another or clinking in a glass of liquid. Collect dried gourds or pods and demonstrate the sounds they make. These sounds could then be used to improvise a 'sound symphony', perhaps adding vocal sounds of various kinds as well.

Write a story with your pupils which can be expressed through sound. For example:

It is Autumn and the wind is blowing through the trees (*vocal sounds by pupils to accompany other pupils moving as trees in the wind*). The leaves are falling and are blown into heaps (*vocal sound of the wind, plus crunch of dried leaves or dried grass being shaken*). It begins to rain (*vocal 'pitter patter' plus sound of shaker or filled container, plus the wind sound*). A boy comes along the road and his shoes are very wet with rain (*vocal 'squelch squelch', plus 'pitter patter', plus shakers and rain sounds*) . . . (*And so on, building up the story and sounds as you and your pupils choose*).

You may decide to use musical instruments only to portray a story. For example:

It is midnight in the village on the hill and the church clock chimes (*chime bar*). Everything is very still, everyone is asleep. It begins to snow softly (*glockenspiel notes or chime bars played slowly and softly*). Suddenly the silence is broken by the sound of a clatter of hooves (*castanets or rhythm sticks*) and the jingle of harness bells (*sleigh bells or tambourines*). It's Father Christmas with presents for all the children asleep in the village. Down the chimneys he goes and up he comes again (*downwards and upwards slides on the xylophone*). Off he goes again to another village (*castanets and bells, loud at first and getting quieter and quieter*). All is quiet again, everyone is still asleep and only the snow falls softly on the houses (*glockenspiel notes played slowly and softly*).

Your pupils will be thrilled to produce the story in sound. It will aid them in the sensitive use of the instruments, help their understanding of a story, lengthen their concentration span, and increase enjoyment of a group activity.

Vocal imitations of instruments

Provide a selection of instruments for your pupils – bells, drums, maracas, triangles, chime bars, finger cymbals, etc. Let each person choose an instrument and play it, then copy the sound it makes vocally. This can aid pupils who have speech difficulties and encourage those who are reticent to attempt making sounds. For those who are able to copy the sounds readily it can be developed into an interesting activity by gradually increasing the difficulty. Ask pupils at random to make their particular sound or to make the sound of the person to the left or right of them. You could conduct a 'vocal orchestra' by indicating one pupil who will make his sound and then another who makes his, and so on.

Sound into action

Begin with your pupils seated on the floor in a circle. Suggest that one at a time they pick up an instrument and walk or dance to the rhythm they play on it. Soon the whole group will be involved in playing and moving and will tend to relate to each other and the sounds that are made as a whole. This may be difficult for some pupils to comprehend at first, depending on their ability. With your aid and with the aid of other helpers they will gradually realise the freedom of such an activity and enter into the spirit of it.

Drama productions

The activities so far described in this chapter not only make enjoyable individual sessions but can be a preparation for your pupils so that they will be able to take part in drama productions. Such productions will of course require far more practice and polish than group sessions without an audience. The following are outlines of plays which you may wish to try for yourself or which will give you ideas for combining music with drama.

THE EMPEROR AND THE NIGHTINGALE

This play was acted by about 35 mentally handicapped people who are in their teens and twenties, for an audience of parents and friends. A few members of the group are mildly handicapped, some moderately handicapped and the rest are severely mentally handicapped. Only one person who took part is in a wheelchair, although others have additional physical handicaps.

The group meets one evening a week for two hours. It took many months of rehearsals to prepare the play for presentation, and grew out of weekly sessions which everyone had enjoyed and which had prepared them for the concentrated work which was necessary. The play was staged in the round in a large hall. The audience were very close to the performers and therefore very much part of the story. Spot lights shone into the circle. The costumes used were as simple as possible but very effective – the soldiers wore dark trousers and white shirts with hired uniform jackets and caps, the emperor looked regal in a long cape and crown, the ladies of the court wore long dresses and crowns, the two nightingales (the 'real' and the clockwork) wore tights and hired bird suits . . . and so on. The drama teacher, Penny Sanderson, who had adapted the story, acted as narrator, standing to one side of the circle. The play began in semi-darkness with one spot light ready to pick out a kneeling figure with bowed head who represented the rising sun.

The Play

NARRATOR: The night is ending and the Nightingale sings his final song. He flies to his rest.

Other birds begin their early morning song, then slowly the sun comes up on this special day. It is the King's birthday.

(*Music*: Thus Spake Zarathustra *by Richard Strauss.*)

(*The spot light shines dimly on the kneeling figure and, as the music builds, he rises and the light increases. Arrayed in a bright cloak he raises his arms one at a time and then both together, then steps onto one low step and, as the music reaches its climax, steps up again with outstretched arms.*)

NARRATOR: In the palace grounds the gardeners are busy getting everything ready.

They dig (*As each activity is mentioned,*
and *groups of pupils perform the*
rake *actions accompanied by appro-*
and *priate sounds.*)
clip
and
mow.

The Princess comes out to pick flowers for her father.

(*The Princess mimes picking and smelling the flowers while the tune* English Country Garden *is played on a glockenspiel.*)

The Prince gathers fruit and vegetables for the King's banquet.

(*The Prince mimes picking the fruit and gathering the vegetables while appropriate sounds are made on instruments.*)

NARRATOR: The palace guards march in the birthday parade and his majesty inspects the soldiers.

(The King stands and watches as a group of pupils dressed as soldiers march to the sound of military music. They march to and fro and around within the circle and then line up in front of the King for inspection. After the inspection one of the soldiers shouts: Three cheers for His Majesty! *They all cheer raising their caps.)*

(Music: Colonel Bogey *by Kenneth Alford.)*

Scene Two: In the Palace

NARRATOR: Inside the palace everyone is preparing for a grand party.

(Music: The Flight of the Bumble Bee *by Rimsky-Korsakov.)*

Some dust and polish.

Others cook delicious food – cakes, jellies, sandwiches and pies.

(Music: sound effects on instruments to accompany cooking.)

NARRATOR: The room and the food are ready, so everyone takes a bath before dressing for the party.

(Mime of bathing and hair washing by pupils to sounds of water splashing and finally gurgling down the drain.)

NARRATOR: The royal family are ready for the party.

(King and Queen, Prince and Princess enter to regal music and walk slowly to their thrones.)

(Music: Trumpet Voluntary *by Jeremiah Clarke.)*

NARRATOR: Many people bring beautiful presents to the King, but the King is already so rich that none of the gifts pleases him.

(Slowly the pupils enter, walk one at a time to the royal group and present their gifts, bow and then move to edge of circle where they sit, ready for the party to begin. The King looks bored and turns his head away from the presents.)

(Music: Trumpet Voluntary *by Jeremiah Clarke.)*

NARRATOR: The royal family and their guests dance, eat and drink but the King is fed up.

(Music: live or recorded mediaeval dance music, Danse Royale (1) French 13th Century. One or more pupils stand up and dance gracefully to the music as the rest clap in time to it and some shake tambourines.)

NARRATOR: Just as the night is ending the little Nightingale sings a wonderful song and, hearing it, his majesty is really happy for the first time.

(One pupil dressed as a nightingale 'flies' around the room to a lilting tune on the flute or other instrument.)

(Music: if live music is not available play Adagio and Variation for Flute *from ballet music to* Ascanio *by Saint-Saëns, using variation.)*

NARRATOR: The King commands the guests to catch the bird but it escapes, wanting to be free.

(Two or three pupils follow the nightingale, but it evades them and disappears outside the circle.)

NARRATOR: The King is unhappy again.

(He acts out his sadness and the Queen attempts to comfort him.)

NARRATOR: While all the court sleeps some clever villagers make a clockwork nightingale.

(Two or three pupils enter with another pupil who is dressed in a rather gaudy bird suit. They mime hammering, cutting and sawing to 'make' the bird, accompanied by sounds made on wood blocks, rhythm sticks, etc.)

NARRATOR: They bring it to the palace where it sings and dances for the King – but it has to be wound up often.

(Bird moves clumsily to live music on a clarinet or other instrument – then the music slows and stops, as does the bird. It is rewound to the sound of castanets and moves off again.)

(Music: if live music is not available use middle section of The Young Prince and the Young Princess *from* Scheherazade *by Rimsky-Korsakov.)*

NARRATOR: The King is delighted and everyone comes to see the great mechanical bird.
(*It continues to move and be rewound and the King shows it off to everyone.*)

NARRATOR: It sings and dances every day but slowly it becomes rusty – until one terrible day it stops.
(*Much clicking and creaking until it stands unable to move.*)

NARRATOR: His Majesty is broken hearted and becomes seriously ill.
(*The King lies back on his throne.*)

NARRATOR: The Queen gives him medicine, but he gets worse. The Prince and Princess try to make him laugh. Everyone begins to worry and some courtiers start to cry.
(*Much miming of medicine taking, attempts to make him laugh and sorrow when he does not respond.*)

NARRATOR: A doctor comes to the bedside to examine the King and finds that he is dying.
(*The King is laid on the floor or a low bed and a 'doctor' comes and listens to his heart – 'beat, beat, beat, beat' getting fainter on the drum.*)

NARRATOR: People tip-toe to the bedside to take a final look at his Majesty.
(*Music*: Pavane for a Dead Infanta *by Ravel.*)

NARRATOR: Night comes and just when everyone is giving up hope, a beautiful sound is heard which fills the room. The little Nightingale flies to the royal bedside and sings and sings.
(*The music begins and the Nightingale 'flies' in, up to the King, around the room and to and fro in front of the King.*)

NARRATOR: Slowly the King sits up, better and happy. The Nightingale promises to sing nightly in the palace. Now his Majesty and everyone in the palace must sleep. They sing a lullaby before they go happily to sleep.
(*Music: All join in singing* Goodnight *song by the Beatles.*)

NARRATOR: And the King and Queen, the Prince and Princess and all the people live happily ever after.
The End

We found that the music played a very important part in the play. It not only added to the atmosphere but played a vital role in the response of the pupils to the action. For example, it set the mood for each scene and the tempo at which it should proceed: the bustle and rush of the preparations, or the sadness and slow movements for the 'death bed' scene. It also aided the pupils to keep up a given activity without further verbal prompt. The music itself would cue the desired activity and they would know that it was time to alter their activity when the music stopped.

Another play in which music played a vital role for the pupils was *The Sleeping Beauty*. This was presented to parents and friends prior to the advent of the drama club. It developed from an idea by speech therapist Peggy Pritchett who wanted to encourage some of her pupils with their speech. Together with occupational therapist Jean Cooper, she practised for many hours with the pupils. Music for the play had to be chosen with great care so that the pupils would know exactly what they should be doing at any given time. The speech therapist took care of all the speaking parts and the occupational therapist took charge of the music. It was found preferable if one person cared for music, as it was used as a cue, rather than that the person nearest to the tape recorder should be asked to switch it on during rehearsals. Live music was not available for this particular play but would be very effective if there were musicians available to take part.

THE SLEEPING BEAUTY
Cast List

King	Good Fairy	Cook	Six good wizards
Queen	Wicked Wizard	Jester	Six dance wizards
Prince	Old Woman	Bear	Herald
Princess	Chamberlain	Doctor	Nurse

Act 1, Scene 1
Stage set – Scene 1
Thrones for King and Queen
Crib for baby
Props: invitations for the christening.
(*Fanfare.*)

HERALD: In the palace of the King and Queen.
(*Enter King and Queen with Nurse.*)

QUEEN: Bring me the baby princess.

NURSE: Yes your Majesty (curtseys).
(*Takes baby from cradle and hands her to the Queen.*)

QUEEN: Rock-a-bye baby . . . (*sings.*)
Send for my Chamberlain. (*The Nurse curtseys and goes out.*)
We shall invite all the fairies and wizards to the christening.
(*Enter Chamberlain carrying invitations. Bows to the King and Queen.*)

QUEEN: Send out the invitations for the Princess Nora's christening.

CHAMBERLAIN: At once, Your Majesty.
(*Exit Chamberlain. He drops one invitation but does not notice.*)
End of Scene 1

Act 1, Scene 2
Stage set – Scene 2
As Scene 1, plus table for the cake at the side of the stage.
Props: Wands for dancing wizards, gifts for good wizards, cake, special wands for Good Fairy and Wicked Wizard.
(*Fanfare.*)

HERALD: The Christening Party for the Princess.
(*The King and Queen are seated on thrones. Beside them, Nurse, Jester and Cook. Enter Chamberlain.*)

CHAMBERLAIN: The wizards will dance for your Majesty.
(*Bows and stands beside the King.*)
(*Wizards' music: sprightly tune with mystic*

flavour, eg. In the Hall of the Mountain King *from* Peer Gynt *by Grieg.*)

(*Enter the Wizards who dance. After the dance they bow to the King and Queen and exeunt.*)

QUEEN: Cook, bring in the cake.

(*The Cook bows and brings cake.*)

QUEEN: Ah, delicious!

KING: Ah, how lovely!

(*The Cook carries cake to the side of the stage.*)

CHAMBERLAIN: The Good Wizards, Your Majesty.

(*Music: Strong regular beat, eg.* Montagues and Capulets *from* Romeo and Juliet, *by Prokofiev.*)

(*The good wizards enter one at a time and bow to the King and Queen, each presenting his gift to the baby in the crib.*)

(*After the last wizard has presented his gift, enter the Wicked Wizard to sound effects – electronic music.*)

WICKED WIZARD: (*Points to the King and Queen.*) You did not invite me to the party, so now I shall curse the Princess.

KING *and* QUEEN: Oh no! We are sorry. Your invitation was lost.

W. WIZARD: Too late! The Princess will prick her finger on a spinning wheel when she is 16 years old and she will die! (*Laughs.*)

(*All show horror. Queen and Nurse cry, King comforts them.*)

(*Music: The Dance of the Sugar Plum Fairy from the* Nutcracker Suite *by Tchaikovsky.*)

GOOD FAIRY: She will not die. She will only sleep for 100 years until a Prince wakes her with a kiss.

W. WIZARD: We will see! (*Exit with a laugh and to the sound of electronic music.*)

QUEEN: Burn up all the spinning wheels in the land!

CHAMBERLAIN: At once, your Majesty!

End of Act 1

Act 2
Stage set – Act 2

Thrones
Spinning wheel and chair
Soft cushion for Princess to fall onto
(*Fanfare.*)

HERALD: The Princess is 16 years old.
(*Old Woman sitting at spinning wheel, slightly off centre of stage. She is spinning.*)
(*Music: a spinning song*, Song without words no. 34 in C *by Mendelssohn.*)
(*Enter Princess. She looks around the stage before seeing the Old Woman.*)

PRINCESS: (*Points to the spinning wheel.*) What is that?

WOMAN: A spinning wheel, my dear.

PRINCESS: Please let me try it.

WOMAN: Of course, my dear. Sit down beside me.
(*Old Woman shows her how to turn the wheel. As she is spinning she pricks her finger.*)

PRINCESS: Oh, I have pricked my finger! (*Screams, holds her head and falls to the floor as if she is dead.*)
(*Enter Wicked Wizard with a laugh and to the sound of electronic music.*)

W. WIZARD: Now you have pricked your finger – you will die!
(*Enter King and Queen with Jester, Nurse, Chamberlain. King and Queen run to the Princess.*)

QUEEN: Doctor! DOCTOR!
(*Enter Doctor who listens to her heart with a stethoscope. He shakes his head.*)
(*Music*: The Dance of the Sugar Plum Fairy *from the* Nutcracker Suite *by Tchaikovsky.*)
(*Enter Good Fairy.*)

GOOD FAIRY: She is not dead, but must sleep for one hundred years. The whole castle must sleep with her. (*Waves her wand over all. Everyone falls asleep – the King and Queen on their thrones and the others on the floor.*)

GOOD FAIRY: The spell will be broken when a Prince wakes her with a kiss.

W. WIZARD: My curse is broken!
(*Exit with angry stamp and shouts. Breaks his wand. Electronic music.*)
End of Act 2

Act 3, Scene 1
Props – Scene 1
Hobby horse for the Prince
Sword
(*Fanfare.*)

HERALD: Near the palace, one hundred years later.
(*Trees on stage – pupils dressed as such – bend and wave to the music.*)
(*Music: quiet section from* William Tell Overture *by Rossini.*)
(*Enter the Prince on his horse. He rides up and down and looks through the trees.*)

PRINCE: I must get through the trees to the castle in the forest.
(*He dismounts and attempts to pass through the trees. They will not let him pass.*)

PRINCE: (*Draws his sword and cuts down the trees.*)
(*Music: final section of* William Tell)
(*He remounts his horse and rides through the trees and exit.*)
End of Scene 1

Act 3, Scene 2
Stage set – Scene 2
Bed for Princess
Thrones
(*Fanfare, very soft.*)

HERALD: The Prince finds his way into the palace.
(*Music; quiet dreamy music,* Träumerei *by Schumann*)
(*The Princess is asleep on the bed. The King and Queen and others are also asleep. Some*

snore gently. Enter the Prince. He looks around until he sees the Princess.)

PRINCE: How beautiful she is! I must wake her.
(*Takes her hand and kisses her on the cheek. The Princess wakes and he helps her up.*)

PRINCESS: (*Rubs her eyes.*) Oh, thank you. You have broken the spell.
(*The King and Queen and others wake up.*)

PRINCE: (*Bows to King and Queen.*) May I marry the Princess Nora?

KING *and* QUEEN: Yes! Chamberlain, arrange the wedding.

CHAMBERLAIN: At once, Your Majesty (*bows*).
End of Scene 2

Act 3, Scene 3
(*Fanfare.*)

HERALD: Our story comes to an end and we have come to say farewell to you.
(*Music: military marches by Sousa.*)
(*Actors come forward to bow, King and Queen first, rest of actors follow.*)
  Fade music when all except the Prince and Princess have taken their bow. Play the Wedding March. *The Prince and Princess walk from the back of the hall to the front and join the rest of the cast to take their bow. At this time the Princess is wearing a wedding gown.*)
(*Final bow to the last bars of the* 1812 Overture *by Tchaikovsky.*)
The End

Performance
The play was a great success but involved much hard work by the pupils as well as those directing it. If you have the use of a hall with a stage, lighting and curtains it is a great advantage, but our performance took place on a small stage with make-shift curtains. The music had been pre-recorded in the correct order and two tape recorders were used, one used for the fanfare and the final music. One pupil whose voice could not be

heard in a hall recorded her part (the Good Fairy) ahead of time. She spoke in the play, while her voice was also played on the tape recorder. The Bear, who had not been scripted, appeared from time to time, rolling over in front of the stage to entertain the audience. He had this part because of his love of applause and of acting in this way.

THE PIED PIPER

This play has not been performed by the pupils for whom it was written. They began to learn the story and act out the scenes from it, really enjoying it all, especially when the rats invaded. However, to make it into a public performance with the particular pupils involved proved to be over ambitious. It has been performed by pupils who are less severely mentally handicapped, in a slightly different form and with different music. Your pupils may be interested in performing it and you can adapt the material to suit them. This version is freely adapted from Robert Browning's original poem *The Pied Piper of Hamelin*.

The Play

NARRATOR: Hamelin Town's in Brunswick
By famous Hanover City.
The River Weser deep and wide
Washes its wall on the Southern side
A pleasanter spot you never spied . . .

(*Enter women who sit beside the river with their babies, spread out a picnic beside the river or walk into the town with baskets.*)
(*Music:* Song 1 *hummed by pupils or played and sung by pupils and helpers.*)

(La) -

(La) -

NARRATOR: But when begins my ditty
            Almost five hundred years ago
            To see the townsfolk suffer so
            From vermin was a pity.
            RATS!
            They fought the dogs and killed the cats
            And bit the babies in their cradles
(Rats run over to the women by the river and attack the babies.)
            And ate the cheeses out of the vats
            And licked the soup from the cook's own ladles
(Rats run towards the town and eat the cheeses, etc.)
            Stole and ate till they got fat
            Made a nest inside her hat
(Take cook's hat and mime making it into a nest.)
            And even spoiled the women's chat
            By drowning their speaking
            With shrieking and squeaking
            In fifty different sharps and flats.
(Music: background of confused sounds played while the 'rat' section is read. At the end, all join in with singing Song 2, 'Rats'.)

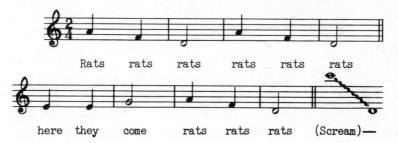

Rats   rats   rats   rats   rats   rats

here   they   come   rats   rats   rats   (Scream)—

Additional verses:

Help, help, help,	What shall we do?
Help, help, help,	What shall we do?
Here they come,	Here they come
Help, help, help!	What shall we do?
Scream ———————	Scream ———————

NARRATOR: At last the people in a body
To the Town Hall came flocking.
'Tis clear' they cried, 'our Mayor's a Noddy;
And as for our corporation – shocking!'

(*Chants of* 'Mayor OUT!' *and* 'Shocking' *from a group of towns folk.*)

The Mayor had no good idea –
An hour he sat and thought.
To the people it was clear
The rats would not be caught
With help from their Mayor.
It really wasn't fair!

(*Everyone sits down to think and the Mayor scratches his head.*)

At last the Mayor did complain,
'It's easy to bid one rack one's brain –
I'm sure my poor head aches again.
I've scratched it so and all in vain!
Oh for a trap, a TRAP! A TRAP!'
Just as he said this what should hap
At the chamber door but a gentle tap.
'Bless us,' cried the Mayor, 'what's that?'
'Anything like the sound of a rat
Makes my heart go pit-a-pat!'

(*The Mayor leaps up looking scared. Song 3 is sung by the Mayor or pre-recorded by him, or sung for him if he cannot sing it.*)

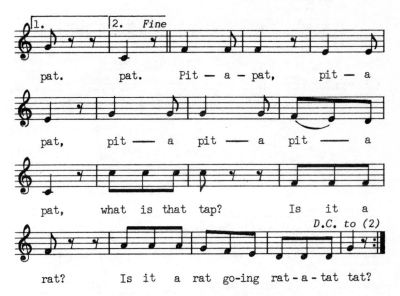

pat. pat. Pit — a — pat, pit — a

pat, pit — a pit — a pit — a

pat, what is that tap? Is it a

D.C. to (2)

rat? Is it a rat go-ing rat - a - tat tat?

(*The second time this song is sung the people join in with:*
        Anything like the sound of a rat
        Makes his heart go pit-a-pat.*)

NARRATOR: 'Come in' – the Mayor cried, looking bigger
              And in did come the strangest figure!
              He himself was tall and thin
              With sharp eyes, each like a pin,
              And light loose hair and beard on chin
              But lips where smiles went out and in.
              He walked up to the Mayor's table
              And 'Please your honour' said he, 'I'm able
              By way of a secret tune to draw
              All creatures living beneath the sun,
              That creep or swim or fly or run,
              After me as you never saw!
              And I mostly use my charm
              On creatures that do people harm –
              The bat and toad and spider and viper
              And people call me the Pied Piper.'
(*The Mayor and Pied Piper mime this and then the Pied Piper
sings* Song 4.)

Lis — ten, lis — ten, while I play,

I can charm those who harm.

Lis — ten, lis — ten, while I play

tunes that bring peace and calm.

Lis — ten, lis — ten, while I play.

I can charm those who harm — the

bat, the toad and spi - der and vi-per — and

peo —— ple call me the PIED PI — PER.

(*The second time this song is sung the people sing:*
Listen, listen while he plays,
He can charm those who harm.
Listen, listen while he plays,
Tunes that bring peace and calm.
The bat and toad and spider and viper
And people call him – the PIED PIPER.)

NARRATOR: 'If I can rid the town of rats
  Will you give me a thousand pounds?'
  'Five thousand,' was the Mayor's reply.
  And then with a sparkle in his eye
  Into the street the Piper stept,
  Smiling first a little smile,
  As if he knew what magic slept
  In his quiet pipe the while.
  Then to blow the pipe his lips he wrinkled
  And green and blue his sharp eyes twinkled
  And before three shrill notes the pipe uttered
  You heard as if an army muttered;
  And the muttering grew to a grumbling
  And the grumbling grew to a mighty rumbling
  And out of the houses rats came tumbling.

(*Music; tune of pipes. Drum roll or several drums growing in sound.*)

  Great rats, small rats, lean rats, old rats,
  Brown rats, black rats, grey rats, bold rats.
  Sad old plodders, gay young friskers,
  Fathers, mothers, uncles, cousins,
  Flicking their tails and twitching whiskers.
  Families by tens and dozens,
  Brothers, sisters, husbands, wives –
  Followed the Piper for their lives.

(*Rats could appear and reappear around an object or through curtains so that there seem to be many more.*)

  From street to street he piped advancing
  And step by step they followed dancing
  Until they came to the River Weser
  Where in all plunged and perished
  And disappeared for ever!

  You should have heard the Hamelin people
  Ringing the bells till they rocked the steeple.

(*Music:* Song 5 *repeated more than once, followed by the playing of glockenspiels, chime bars and sleigh bells while the townsfolk dance around. Repeat the song again to the accompaniment of the bells.*)

NARRATOR: 'Go,' cried the Mayor, 'and get long poles,
Poke out the nests and block up the holes.
Get the carpenters around
And leave in our town
Not a trace

Of the rats!' When suddenly, up the face
Of the Piper popped in the market place,
With a 'First if you please, my thousand pounds.'
A thousand pounds! The Mayor was a cheat,
He thought he'd got the Piper beat.
He wouldn't give up any money
The rats were gone – how very funny!
'I won't pay you so do your worst,
Go blow your pipe until you burst!'
(*Music*: Song 6, *plus much more laughter and jeering by the crowd towards the Pied Piper.*)

He won't pay you, Ha, Ha, Ha!

You'll stay poor, He, He, He!

He won't pay you we are sure.

Ha, Ha, He, He, Ho, Ho, Ho!

NARRATOR: Once more he stept into the street
And to his lips again
Laid his long pipe of smooth straight cane;
And as he blew three notes so sweet
There was a rushing that seemed like a bustling
Of merry crowds pushing and shoving and hustling,
Small feet were pattering, wooden shoes clattering,
Little hands clapping and little tongues chattering.
Then out on the street the children came running.

All the little boys and girls
With shining eyes and teeth like pearls,
Tripping and skipping, ran merrily after
The wonderful music with shouting and laughter.
(*Sound effects of the running and chattering while this is said.*
Music: Song 7 *sung by or for the children.*)

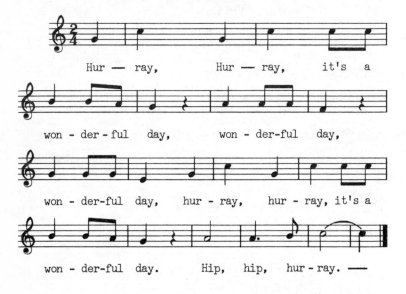

Hur — ray,   Hur — ray,   it's   a
won - der - ful   day,   won - der - ful   day,
won - der - ful   day,   hur - ray,   hur - ray, it's a
won - der - ful   day.   Hip,   hip,   hur - ray. —

NARRATOR: The Mayor was dumb and the people stood
As if they were changed into blocks of wood,
Unable to move a step or cry
To the children merrily skipping by –
(*Music*: Song 8 *sung by everyone quietly while they stand stiffly,*
or recorded and played while they stand like statues.)

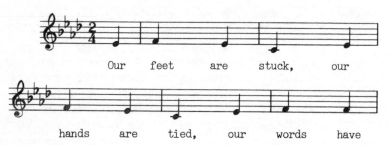

Our   feet   are   stuck,   our
hands   are   tied,   our   words   have

NARRATOR: They could only follow with the eye
            The little children skipping by.
            Off they ran with tapping feet
            After the Piper down the street
            To where the river rolled its water
            Right in the way of their sons and daughters . . .
            However he turned off to the West
            And after him the children pressed
            On and on to the mountain side
            Where suddenly it opened wide
            As if a cave was suddenly hollowed.
            The Piper entered and the children followed.
            And when all were in to the very last
            The door of the mountain side shut fast.

            Did I say all? NO! One was lame
            And he could not dance the whole of the way.
            He slowly, sadly returned in shame –
            Shouted out – 'The Mayor's to blame.
            He's the one who sent them away,
            He's the one who'll have to pay.'
            Slowly all the people unfroze
            Except the Mayor – who kept his pose.
            The Mayor still dumb stood all alone –
            A statue for ever, carved out of stone.

(*End with the Mayor as a statue and the people all pointing at him, for several seconds. Then all turn and take their bow, followed by the rats and the children who reappear with the Piper.*)

The End

There are many well known stories that can easily be turned into plays. Some are easier to perform than others. You and your pupils may enjoy considering which of their favourite stories could best be acted. Perhaps they will be able to help in writing songs to accompany a play or decide how a story can be adapted. If you are working one-to-one with your child or pupil you can still have a lot of fun taking it in turn to act the various characters which appear in the three plays that I have suggested, or in stories that you are reading together.

10: MUSIC IN WORSHIP

The days are gone when attendance at church was compulsory for people who, because of a physical or mental handicap, lived in a hospital, home or hostel. One hospital I visited, which is home for hundreds of mentally handicapped people, has a huge church in its grounds. This was built at a time when the hospital had many more people living there, most of whom now live in the community. Today, half the church is closed off in order to provide an additional activity area for the network of training units available to the residents. The remaining part of the church is quite large enough for all those who choose to worship.

Sometimes the question is asked, 'Do handicapped people today want the opportunity to worship, and do mentally handicapped people understand what it is about?' Let me share an experience with you that surprised me some time ago. During a Makaton signing session I happened to say to a pupil, 'Put your hands together – as if you're saying prayers – and . . .' He stopped me in mid sentence by excitedly waving his arms and making sounds. He pointed to the floor, put his hands together and then pointed upwards. He wanted to discuss with me his understanding of prayer. From replies to questions (he nods or shakes his head) and through signs, he told me that he believed in God and that he knew he could pray to Him and that God would answer and help him. Since then I have found that he loves to listen to anyone singing hymns. His face lights up with joy when he hears hymns such as 'Jesus loves me' and 'All things bright and beautiful'. He is particularly fond of Christmas carols, but these he firmly links to Christmas and the receiving of presents rather than to any spiritual aspect.

This young man is in his early twenties and is severely mentally and physically handicapped. He seems an unlikely person to respond to anything spiritual. He is renowned for his outbursts of temper and can scream for hours on end. If given what he wants when he wants it he demands more, and if denied a request for good reasons will continue to misbehave until he becomes tired of his own behaviour and begins to sign 'sorry' to everyone. One day on an outing to a park he became annoyed by something and caused a great disturbance. When I eventually spoke to him (I was not looking after him on this occasion) he reluctantly agreed to stop screaming long enough to listen. I talked to him about the beautiful things he could see around him. 'Who made these things for us?' I asked him. He pointed upwards. We continued our discussion about the trees, flowers and the nearby river and how wonderful it is to have such beautiful things to look at. I asked him if he would like to ask God to take away his anger and make him feel better (although quiet by now he was still rocking hard and on the verge of screaming). He nodded his agreement and put his hands together without prompt. I prayed a simple prayer for him and he relaxed. We rejoined the group. He had become perfectly relaxed and calm and enjoyed the rest of the day and the coach trip home. Several people asked me what we had been talking about and what I had promised him to bring about such a change – but we kept the secret to ourselves lest anyone think it an unlikely tale and break the calm that had been established.

A service is provided every few weeks for the residents where the young man lives. He very much enjoys these, but sometimes is unable to attend because of his bad behaviour on that particular day; to take him out somewhere special would appear to him as a reward for being disruptive. When being well behaved he is rewarded by outings and special things to do. The service, conducted by a group of people with the padré, is very effective, avoiding long sermons and providing plenty of singing. The young people come from local churches and play and sing gospel choruses and action songs. It is recognised as a service and not just another entertainment; those who attend will often say to the padré, 'See you at church,' or if unable to speak will put their hands together and then point in the direction of the building where the service is normally held.

Irene is now in her late teens. She is severely mentally handicapped and wears calipers to aid her walking. She attends church with her parents and younger sister. While her parents enjoy the adult Bible study group she attends a class with children much younger than herself who more closely match her mental age. The children have accepted her despite the fact that she is so much taller than they are. They have always insisted that she 'say' a memory verse. The day she actually managed to put two words together caused great jubilation. She loves joining in the action songs. This arrangement has the added advantage that the younger children are learning to understand and accept a person who is mentally handicapped. During the family service which follows, Irene can stay in a room adjoining the church if the service proves too long for her. As the service is relayed there, mum and dad have always been able to enjoy the sermon while Irene takes some exercise, and she can then listen to and enjoy the hymns. Having the backing of a whole church like this can be a great help to parents and to the handicapped person who might otherwise feel very isolated and lonely.

Everyone experiences doubts, fears and depression at certain times in their lives. Handicapped people can be even more vulnerable to such feelings as they are limited in what they can do and where they can go, or are frustrated by lack of speech, by the inability to fulfil their ambitions or by the thoughtlessness of other people. Many find an answer to their need in worship. They are able to put their trust in a divine person who is interested in their problems. They can worship together with other people and make friends in a caring society. There are also Christian groups and holiday fellowships which cater particularly for people with a handicap. It can be a tremendous relief to get together with others who have experienced similar problems and to discuss, pray and sing about one's faith. Hymns and choruses are particularly uplifting for handicapped people as they often express the problems and anxiety of life and then provide answers to these problems.

One of the Psalms in the Old Testament of the Bible speaks of music in praising God:

> Praise the Lord!
> Praise him for the mighty things he has done.
> Praise his supreme greatness.

Praise him with trumpets.
Praise him with harps and lyres.
Praise him with drums and dancing.
Praise him with harps and flutes.
Praise him with cymbals.
Praise him with loud cymbals.
Praise the Lord, all living creatures
Praise the Lord!

(Psalm 150, *Good News Bible*)

Fanny Crosby, who was blind, wrote many beautiful hymns brimming over with praise and joy, despite her own handicap. For example, the hymn 'Praise Him!':

Praise Him! praise Him! Jesus our blessed Redeemer!
Sing, O earth – His wonderful love proclaim!
Hail Him! hail Him! highest arch-angels in glory;
Strength and honour give to His holy name!
Like a shepherd, Jesus will guard His children,
In His arms He carries them all day long;
Refrain
Praise Him! praise Him! tell of His excellent greatness;
Praise Him! praise Him! ever in joyful song!

and her hymn 'Redeemed! How I love to proclaim it', the third verse of which says:

I think of my blessed Redeemer,
I think of Him all the day long;
I sing, for I cannot be silent;
His love is the theme of my song.

The refrain of her hymn 'Blessed Assurance' is full of happiness:

This is my story, this is my song,
Praising my Saviour all the day long;
This is my story, this is my song,
Praising my Saviour all the day long.

Many other hymns are filled with meaning for those who are seeking help to sustain them through trials and difficulties, such as 'I need Thee every hour':

I need Thee every hour, in joy or pain;
Come quickly and abide, or life is vain.

I need Thee every hour; teach me Thy will;
And Thy rich promises in me fulfil.
Refrain
I need Thee, oh, I need Thee, every hour I need Thee!
Oh, bless me now, my Saviour, I come to Thee.

A hymn which expresses God's care for us whatever comes our way is 'Be not dismayed':

> Be not dismayed whate'er betide,
> God will take care of you;
> Beneath His wings of love abide,
> God will take care of you.
> *Refrain*
> God will take care of you,
> Thro' every day, o'er all the way;
> He will take care of you,
> God will take care of you.

The hymn 'When we walk with the Lord' has a verse which states:

> Not a burden we bear, not a sorrow we share,
> But our toil He doth richly repay;
> Not a grief nor a loss, not a frown nor a cross,
> But is blest if we trust and obey.

A favourite hymn of many people is the beautiful hymn 'Be still my soul', often sung to the tune *Finlandia*:

> Be still my soul: the Lord is on thy side;
> Bear patiently the cross of grief or pain;
> Leave to thy God to order and provide;
> In every change He faithful will remain.
> Be still my soul: thy best, thy heavenly Friend
> Through thorny ways leads to a joyful end.

Think too of the words of the hymn 'What a friend we have in Jesus'. What a comfort it is to sing such beautiful words. Or the hymn 'In the heart of Jesus' which describes the love available to those who seek it.

'O love that will not let me go' has some of the most beautiful words to be found in any hymn book. It is also arranged for choirs and is delightful to listen to:

O joy that seekest me through pain,
I cannot close my heart to Thee;
I trace the rainbow through the rain,
And feel the promise is not vain
That morn shall tearless be.

These are just a few of the wealth of hymns, not to mention gospel choruses, which are to be found in hymn books. Many people have found that the words of particular hymns have a very personal meaning to them and bring them just the right encouragement at the time they need it. The tunes and words linger on in the mind long after a hymn is sung and bring joy and relief into the heart and courage to face the problems of life, whatever they may be.

The blind will be able to see
    and the deaf will hear.
The lame will leap and dance,
    and those who cannot speak will shout for joy.
(Isaiah 35: 5 & 6, *Good News Bible*)

All the hymns quoted are from *The New Advent Hymnal* published by the Stanborough Press Ltd.

IN CONCLUSION

In this book I have shared with you my personal thoughts and feelings on the use of music with handicapped people. I hope that you will have caught a little of my enthusiasm and that you will find ways of sharing your love of music with the people with whom you are working, or with handicapped friends or relatives. The world of music lies at your feet. Do not be afraid to step forward and enjoy it with the people who are special to you.

READING LIST AND SONG BOOKS

Alvin, J. *Music for the Handicapped Child* (2nd edition).
London: Oxford University Press, 1976. (Out of print but still
available in certain libraries.)

Alvin J. *Music for the Autistic Child*. London: Oxford University
Press, 1978.

Appleby, W., Fowler, F. *Sing Together!* (a collection of 100
songs for children) London: Oxford University Press, 1967.

Barratt, S., Hodge, S. (chosen by) *Tinder Box*. A and C Black.

Baxter, K. *Fundamental Activities*. 1993. Video, video notes,
book on music, with movement, design and language
alongside. Part proceeds to Muzika in Romania. From: P.O.
Box 149, Nottingham, NG3 5PU.

Bean, J., Oldfield, A. *Pied Piper* (80 different musical activities
for children and adults with learning disabilities). Cambridge
University Press.

Bell, H. *Abracadabra Guitar!* (folk guitar tutor). A and C
Black.

Beresford-Peirse, S., du Feu, J., Worthington, J., Nordoff, P.
The Goldie Leigh Song Book. London: Nordoff-Robbins
Music Therapy Centre.

Birkenshaw-Fleming, L. *Come on everybody, let's sing.* (Over a
hundred songs and 85 poems for children). From: Gordon V.
Thompson Music, 85 Scarsdale Road, Unit 104, Don Mills,
Ontario, M3B 2R2, Canada.

Blakeley, P., Gadsby, D., Harrop, B. *Apusskidu* (56 songs
chosen for children). A and C Black.

Braille Music for Beginners. 1987. RNIB, Peterborough.

Bush, R. (chosen by) *The Jolly Herring* (77 songs—folk and
pop). A and C Black.

Clark, C., Chadwick, D. *Clinically Adapted Instruments for the
Multiply Handicapped: a resource book*. Magnamusic-Baton
Inc. 1980. From Schott & Co. Ltd.

Clarkson, G. *Moon Sense* (a musical play for young adults with learning disabilities). Magna Music Baton Inc. Available Schott & Co. Ltd.

Focus. Newsletter for staff working with visual and learning disabled people. RNIB, Peterborough.

Friend, L., Gadsby, D., Harrop, B. *Okki-Tokki-Unga* (action songs chosen for children). A and C Black.

Gadsby, D., Harrop, B. (chosen by) *Harlequin* (44 songs round the year). A and C Black.

Gilbert, J. *Story, Song and Dance* (collection of ideas for improvised drama with music). Cambridge University Press.

Gilbert, J., Davies, L. *Oxford Primary Music* (teacher's notes, songbooks, activity sheets). Oxford University Press.

Goran, U. *Play Guitar Book 1*. Oxford University Press.

Holst, I. *An ABC of Music* (based essential rudiments, harmony and form of music). Oxford University Press.

Kennard, D. *Report on Access to Music for the Physically Handicapped Schoolchild and School Leaver*. From the National Music and Disability Information Service.

Lucas, J. *Beginning Music* (pack of coloured cards to stimulate young or handicapped children to sing, play or create). Taskmaster Ltd.

Maughan, J. *Pitch In!* (how to play simple piano and guitar accompaniments; how to hold, play and make percussion instruments etc.), Oxford University Press.

Miller, N. *Simple Home-made Instruments*. Available from the author: 13 Modena Road, Hove, Sussex, BN3 5QF.

Nordoff, P., Robbins, C. *Children's Playsongs Nos. One to Five*. USA: Theodore Presser. Available from Alfred A. Kalmus.

Nordoff, P., Robbins, C. *Fun for Four Drums*. USA: Theodore Presser, 1968. Available from Alfred A. Kalmus.

Nordoff, P., Robbins, C. *Music Therapy in Special Education*. Magnamusic Baton. Available from Schott & Co. Ltd.

Nordoff, P., Robbins, C. *Therapy in Music for Handicapped Children*. London: Gollancz, 1971.

Ockelford, A., *Music and Visually Impaired Children* (some notes for the guidance of teachers), 1991. RNIB, Peterborough.

Orff, G. *The Orff Music Therapy*. London: Schott. 1980.

Pearson, D., *Up, Up, and Away* (50 songs with poems, games

and stories suitable for people with learning difficulties). Oxford University Press. 1987.

Robins, F., Robins, J. *Educational Rhythmics for Mentally and Physically Handicapped Children Part 1* (book and tapes). Switzerland: RA-Verlag. Available from Jennet Robins (see address list). As above, *Part 2*, available from Brothers of Charity, Bawnmore, Limerick, Ireland.

Russell, J. *Graded Activities for Children with Motor Difficulties*. Cambridge University Press.

Sherborne, V. *Developmental Movement for Children*. Cambridge University Press.

Someone's Singing Lord. (59 hymns and songs for children) A and C Black.

Warren, M., Spinks, D. *Songs of Speech* (book and tape). Taskmaster Ltd.

USEFUL ADDRESSES

Achievement and Special Needs for Children and Adults, T.F.H., 76 Barracks Road, Sandy Lane Industrial Estate, Stourport-on-Severn, Worcestershire, DY13 9QB. Tel 0299 827820. Fax 0299 827035. *Electronic organ (similar to Touch-a-Tune) for disabled people, sound boxes, musical instruments, percussion instruments for people without manual dexterity.*

Association of Professional Music Therapists, Administrator: Diana Asbridge, Chestnut Cottage, 38 Pierce Lane, Fulbourn, Cambridge, CB1 5DL. Tel 0223 880377.

British Institute of Learning Disabilities, Information and Resource Centre, Wolverhampton Road, Kidderminster, DY10 3PP. Tel 0562 850251 Fax 0562 851970. *Journal: British Journal of Learning Disabilities (formerly Mental Handicap) and full publication list available from BILD Publications, Frankfurt Lodge, Clevedon Hall, Victoria Road, Clevedon, Avon, BS21 7SJ. Tel 0275 876519.*

British Society for Music Therapy, Administrator: Denize Christophers, 69 Avondale Avenue, East Barnet, Herts., EN4 8NB. Tel 081-368 8879. *Membership open to all whose vocational activities enable them to further the objects of the Society. Publish (jointly with the APMT) the Journal of British Music Therapy.*

Castle Priory, (Spastics Society), Thames Street, Wallingford, Oxfordshire, OX10 0HE. Tel 0491 37551. *Occasional courses on music for people with disabilities.*

Choice Technology and Training, 7 The Rookery, Orton Wistow, Peterborough, PE2 0YT. Tel 0733 23441. Contact: Roger Wilson-Hinds. *Soundbeam.*

Council for Music in Hospitals, Director: Pamela Smith, 74 Queens Road, Hersham, Surrey, KT12 5LW. Tel 0932 252809/252811, Fax 0932 252966. *Professional artists provide concerts in hospitals, NHS Trusts and Day Centres.*

Early Learning Centre: see telephone directory for local centre.

EMS Soundbeam, 87 Mill Hill Road, Norwich, NR2 3DR. Tel 0603 631647. *Soundbeam equipment.*

English Folk Dance and Song Society, Cecil Sharp House, 2 Regent's Park Road, London, NW1 7AY. Tel 071-485 2206.

Guildhall School of Music and Drama, The Registrar, Barbican, London, EC2Y 8DT. Tel 071-628 2571. *One year postgraduate course in Music Therapy (GSMD/York).*

Hope Education Ltd., Orb Mill, Huddersfield Road, Oldham, Lancashire, OL4 2ST. Tel 061-633 6611. Fax 061-633 3431. *Catalogue includes music equipment and sound box.*

High Spirits, 21 Etherley Road, London N15 3AL. Tel 081-800 0156. Contact: Gus Garside. *A group of singers and musicians based at a centre for people with learning disabilities.*

London Music Shop Ltd., Bedwas House Industrial Estate, Bedwas, Newport, Gwent, NP1 8XQ. Tel 0222 865775. *Catalogue of musical instruments.*

Makaton Vocabulary Development Project, Director: Margaret Walker M.Sc. F.C.S.T., 31 Firwood Drive, Camberley, Surrey, GU15 3QD. Tel 0276 61390. *Information on workshops and Makaton Nursery Rhyme video and song book.*

Margaret Morris Movement, Suite 3/4, Hope Street, Glasgow, G2 6AG. Administrator: Jim Hastie. *Exercise, movement and dance classes for people of all ages and disabilities. Write for list of regional representatives around Britain. Operates in fifteen different countries.*

Messenger and Clark, Georgian Lodge, Pious Drove, Upwell, Wisbech, Cambridge, PE14 9AN. Tel 0945 773627 or 0902 895991. *Wooden play equipment, sound boxes, etc.*

Music Education Supplies, 101 Banstead Road South, Sutton, Surrey, SM2 5LH. Tel 081-770 3866. *Catalogue of books and instruments.*

Music Therapy Service, Greenwich Health Authority, Integrated Child Health Services Unit, Music Therapy Department, 4 Wensley Close, Off Court Road, Eltham, London, SE9 5AD, Tel 081-294 1883, ext 8. *Therapy available from a team of qualified Music Therapists (Nordoff-Robbins).*

Music Therapy Diploma Course. University of Bristol, Staff Tutor in Music, Department for Continuing Education, Wills Memorial Building, Queens Road, Bristol, BS8 1HR. Tel 0272 303616. *Part-time, two-year Music Therapy Diploma Course.*

National Music and Disability Information Service, Director: Laura Critchton, Dartington Hall, Totnes, Devon, TQ9 6EJ. Tel 0803 866701.

Natural Movement Association, Pebble Beach House, Strange Garden, Dark Lane, Bognor Regis, W. Sussex, PO21 4RL. Tel 0243 863934. *Courses available. Useful for those working with people with disabilities.*

Nordoff-Robbins Music Therapy Centre, 2 Lissendon Gardens, London NW5 1PP. Tel 071-267 4496. *One year postgraduate course in Music Therapy.*

Nottingham Rehab, Ludlow Hill Road, West Bridgford, Nottingham, NG2 6HD. Tel 0602 452345. Fax 0602 452124. *Catalogue includes musical instruments, books, songs and tapes.*

Premier Percussion Ltd. Bladby Road, Wigston, Leicestershire, LE18 4DF. Tel 0533 773121. Telex 342171. Fax 0533 776627.

Quest Enabling Designs Ltd., Ability House, 242 Gosport Road, Farnham, Hampshire, PO16 0SS. Tel 0329 828444. *Wooden play equipment and sound boxes, etc.*

Resources for Learning Difficulties, The Consortium, Jack Tizard School, Finlay Street, London SW6 6HB. *Publish 'Galaxies' and 'Seaside' for pupils with profound and multiple learning difficulties.*

Robins, Jennet, Educational Rhythmics, Eilweg 4, CH-8634 Hombrechtikon, Switzerland. Tel 055/42 33 66. *Books and tapes available.*

Roehampton Institute, Roehampton Lane, London, SW15 5PU. Tel 081-392 3000. *One year postgraduate music therapy course. Contact the Registrar.*

Rompa, Goyt Side Road, Chesterfield, S40 2PH. Tel 0246 211777. Fax 0246 221812. *Catalogue includes musical instruments, resource material and leisure and therapy products.*

Royal National Institute for the Blind, RNIB, Leisure Services, 224 Great Portland Street, London, W1N 6AA. Tel 071-388 1266 Ex 2350. *Information includes sports, music, arts, broadcasting, museums etc.* RNIB Music Adviser. Tel 081-968 8600. RNIB

Leisure Officer, music. Tel 071-388 1266 Ex 2300. RNIB Customer Services, P.O. Box 173, Peterborough, PE2 6WS. Tel 0345 023153 *(local call cost)*. *Publications orders*.

Royal Society for Mentally Handicapped Children and Adults (MENCAP), 123 Golden Lane, London ECY 0RT. Tel 071-454 0454. *Books and occasional music and movement workshops for those involved with people with disabilities*.

Schott & Co. Ltd., Music Publishers, 48 Great Marlborough Street, London, W1V 2BN. Tel 071-437 1246. Fax 071-437 0263.

Sesame, Christchurch, 27 Blackfriars Road, London, SE1 8NY. Tel 071-633 9690. *Drama and movement for people with learning disabilities*.

Shape London, 1 Thorpe Close, London, W10 5YL. Tel 081-960 9245. *Information on movement and dance*.

SITE, Section for Independence Through Education, The City Lit, Stukeley Street, Drury Lane, London, WC2B 5LJ. Tel 071-831 6908. *Music courses available for people with learning disabilities*.

Taskmaster Ltd., Morris Road, Leicester, LE2 6BR. Tel 0533 704286. Fax 0533 706992. *Catalogue available*.

Tobin Music, The Old Malthouse, Knight Street, Sawbridgeworth, Hertfordshire, CM21 9AX. Tel 0279 726625/722318. *Courses on the Tobin Music System, composing music on computer, Musicolor, colour and music books*.

Ways into Music, 1 Brackenridge, 26 Bracken Hill Lane, Bromley, Kent, BR1 4AJ. Tel 081-313 9148. Contact: Christine Richards. *Workshops, curriculum planning, books with ideas for music in primary and special schools*.

Wheelchair Dance Association, 43 Thurlby Road, Wembley, Middlesex, HA0 4RT. Tel 081-902 5102. Contact: Michael Massey.

Winslow Catalogue, Telford Road, Bicester, Oxon, OX6 0T5. Freephone: 0800 243755. Fax 0869 320040. *Basic music instruments, books on music and on disabilities. Music tapes*.